rural

The worst realities of our age are manufactured realities. It is therefore our task, as creative participants in the universe, to redream our world. The fact of possessing imagination means that everything can be redreamed. Each reality can have its alternate possibilities. Human beings are blessed with the necessity of transformation.

Ben Okri, 'The Human Race is Not Yet Free',
A Way of Being Free (Phoenix : London 1997)

rural

open to all, beginners welcome

[*Based on conversations, actions and reflections*
carried out with mari-aymone DJERIBI]

published by *mermaid turbulence* mmvii

for the RURAL THOUGHT COLLECTIVE

DOMINIC STEVENS

© 2007 *mermaid turbulence*

first published by

mermaid turbulence
annaghmaconway
cloone, leitrim, ireland.

a CIP catalogue record for this title is available from The British Library

ISBN 978-1-901776-01-0

for authorization to reproduce this
book in any part or by any means
please kindly contact the publisher

www.mermaidturbulence.com

rural

open to all, beginners welcome

think

I hereby record a personal journey. I have come to believe that you have to experience something to really understand it, that the things that you can touch or feel, are richer than things read about or imagined. I believe that the people that you can sit down and talk to have more to tell you than statistics. It is only through action that you gain enlightenment.

This journey brought me from an urban life to a rural one, and carries me on as I search for the reality of a rural existence, for what the essence and future of the rural is. The journey is fired by a process of action and reflection ; things are done, objects produced—buildings, installations, photos and essays—the gaps between all these fill up with reflection, conversations, questions, informing and driving further acts.

As I sit here and sift through these essays, written from my own experiences about the people that I have got to know, I wonder where it does leave me, what further actions can be fired from these reflections taken as a set of ideas. *Rural* is the way that I choose to share my findings, hoping to have enriched the discussion about the future of the rural and looking forward to future discussions.

My thanks go to the Arts Council who have, through their awarding of the Kevin Kieran Award allowed me to formalize and expand a process of work and research and allowed me to publish this book. My thoughts go to Kevin Kieran, the first architectural adviser to the Arts Council, a charming and erudite man whom I met only a handful of times before his untimely death. This award was his brainchild, I hope that he would have appreciated and enjoyed what it has allowed me to do.

childhood

I am a child of the suburbs. I grew up with Dublin city centre twenty minutes in one direction, and the countryside twenty minutes in the other. It seemed that I was somehow stranded in the middle, not really a Dubliner, and definitely not from the country. My parents, too, had grown up in the suburbs, I could not even claim urban or rural roots through them either. When asked 'Where do you come from ?' I had to answer with caution, a Dubliner would laugh if I, a kid from Dún Laoghaire, claimed to be from Dublin, though down the country I definitely belonged to Dublin. I observed both camps but seemed to belong nowhere.

The countryside was for days out, for holidays, for leisure. Not having any rural relations to visit, the sites of our holidays were holiday houses or caravans and contact with the rural dwellers, *the locals*, limited to trips to the shop. We were like a family on safari.

My memories of these trips are of grand majestic nature, of wind and rain, wild seas, great beauty, a big natural playground. The people remained mysterious, as mysterious as the country-and-western music which I heard in the shops and bars and which I believed was so called because it came from the west of Ireland.

Like every child, I knew from books that the countryside is the place where farmers live and work, and around me on holidays I did catch glimpses of farmers. What exactly this rural life had to do with me was unclear as even back then in the 1970s vegetables were more often than not from Holland, and heating was powered with oil from the Arabs, not turf from Ireland. The Irish countryside was for the suburban child simply a place for the holidays.

This was underlined in many ways. Bord Faílte promoted this Ireland, natural, old-fashioned, innocent, as did films, books, and of course it was how it seemed to be understood by the large American tourists in loud trousers overheard on buses and trains, the most vocal consumers of this great natural museum.

Rural Ireland seemed in its advertised innocence and backwardness to be dealt with by the *sophisticated, urban, modern Ireland* as a simple child, to be dictated to, sometimes humoured and enjoyed for its simplicity, but not truly part of the contemporary world.

a student

At university, studying to be an architect, we were assigned design projects. Some of these were urban, and some rural. I enjoyed the rural-based projects, where it seemed to me that the architect could respond to great elemental themes, heroic man set against the forces of nature. Modern architecture was as rich in these themes as the other arts : we had 'Falling Water', the house designed by Frank Lloyd Wright, just as literature had *Moby Dick*. In my rural-based projects in college, the land, and the agricultural traces of man on these rural sites, were read as nature, as opposed to my proposed constructs which I understood as artificial. It was me as a child on holiday, me, modern and urbane, and the mountain, a wild stranger.

My graduating thesis was just such a building. Set in the drama of Lough Dan in County Wicklow, it was an outdoor pursuit centre for urban types to enjoy the countryside. The building was made of two identifiable parts, one part was of the site, hewn from rock, containing cavelike spaces, the other a light pre-fabricated frame, a contemporary thing, made in *civilization* and floated over to the site to be anchored to the natural wall that I had delivered from the existing rock.

Thinking back, this wall of cavelike spaces was the first time that the natural became part of something that I was designing, a part of me. The first time my hands were dirtied, metaphorically at any rate.

moving to the countryside

Ten years after graduating, I found myself moving to the country. My wife, mari-aymone DJERIBI, though raised in the suburbs of Paris had a rural father and used to spend a large proportion of her school holidays at her grandmother's in a small village in Franche-Comté. She enjoyed the experience to a large extent, growing up with the firm intention of living in the country at some stage in her life.

Our lease was running out on our flat in the centre of town, we contemplated our next move : urban seemed to mean unfathomable debt, suburban meant debt and unfathomable commuting, while rural was rife with possibility.

11

We thus decided to build ourselves a house, a cheap house, with our own hands, and therefore be able to continue to enjoy the benefits of a debt-free life. On a pragmatic level, the countryside seemed to be the place to do this (cheaper sites), so off we headed into rural Ireland, Leitrim to be exact, to build our house.

It is always difficult to imagine a building where previously there was none, for architects, I think, as much as for anyone else, and as we moved on to our site, the house that was in my head remained very much an abstract thing. We camped, secured hedges to keep out neighbouring cows, and begun to set out where the foundations would be, marks on the ground to be dug, concrete poured, and then a large stack of timber which had this sweet smell that freshly cut timber does. A frame, then an enclosure, onwards and onwards we worked.

Somehow the act of field becoming building became more akin to gardening. Progress, sometimes slow, sometimes quick, was dependent on physical work and ingenuity and like in gardening a lot was also left to the goodwill of things outside of our contol. The building that was appearing seemed to me to be more a measure of work done than an act of creation, it wasn't being conjured up out of the ether, rather it was flesh and blood, a real thing, imperfect and very hard won.

I had entered a world where it seemed more creative to dig the ground than to think about digging it. I learnt that there is a logic in the physicality of doing.

The beauty of rural Ireland.

people

The landscape where we were building our house, has, like most Irish landscapes a scattering of houses, with each house on a small farm. What this meant was that just as we were out in our field making our house, our neighbours were out, cutting grass, moving and foddering cattle, mending roofs, fixing fences and clearing drains. Just as we were altering our land, they were constantly altering theirs. We were all doing the same thing, simply following logic based on economics and politics, mixed with a measure of tradition and common sense.

These people, who we now live amongst, know why their particular landscape is in the exact form that it is, to them a lot comes down to common sense. This is a hard-won knowledge that is based on stories and anecdotes

The beauty of rural Ireland.

forests cleared
stones collected
crops sown
weeds suppressed
crops harvested
hay made
manure collected
fertilizer spread
dwellings built
ditches dug
hedgerows grown
walls built
roads made
forests planted
barns erected

Ireland's rural landscape
is as man-made as the
skyline of Manhattan.

attached to the memories of people long gone. Although imbued with very useful knowledge they do not have the arrogance of some scientists, they are still learning as they work, their precious knowledge a process that they took on and will hand on as they go. Not that country people necessarily have a deep connection with nature, rather that those who work the land have formed this landscape with countless years of work, that all that came before them are present to their mind. They know that no matter how much you know and hard you work things may still go wrong. 'This drain needs clearing in autumn, if it isn't the water will run down the road and damage it… If you dig too steep a bank there it will slip, but over there, it won't… You need to cut that tree down, otherwise it will blow over with the next storm'…

The work of a people is indivisible from their landscape. Landscape is permanent action, a thing in flux, a result of work. Mari-aymone describes this in terms of the scientific theory expanded in *The Third Policeman* by Flann O'Brien, where the swapping of molecules between the arse of the policeman and the saddle of his bicycle renders one almost indistinguishable from the other.

Our neighbours' fields are full of gorse, we have none. Apparently the man who farmed our land all his life had a hatred of gorse, and a skill and determination with regard to its removal. His passion is made visible on the land.

function

In the past the decisions made about the landscapes around me by its occupants had always been pragmatic, concerned with making a living this year and preparing for the next. Since we have arrived here I have noticed that our neighbours are making decisions responding to legislation and available grants rather than using their own knowledge, we live in a time that the adviser in the suit with a science degree has more authority than a craft built up over hundreds of years.

Padraig, the neighbour who sold us the site, is as good an example as any. Lead by an intelligent response to the land available to him, grants available and possible financial return he has never farmed full time, this he shares with many Leitrim farmers. He has worked at a variety of things since we have known him, steel-door fitting and repairing at first, in the last few years he has driven a lorry delivering animal feed the length and breadth of the country, and at the moment he drives a school bus. He sold us a site from a parcel of land that he inherited from his gorse-hating uncle, on the rest he used to keep cows, then for a while sheep. He now has got out of food production altogether and breeds horses for sale, producing items for the leisure market, non-essentials to be consumed by people with a bit of spending power.

Another neighbour has gone in the other direction and intensified. He has put huge investment into enormous sheds where cattle are raised inside, being fed on meal, silage and hay, through this capital-intensive expansion he can continue to make money producing food, though he is taking a big gamble on the future price of beef offset against the rising price of the oil that intensive farming is so reliant on.

Around me then has changed in the seven years that it has been under my gaze, from being a landscape of cows in fields, to being one with horses, large sheds and empty meadows to be mowed for silage, and always less and less people working the land.

Farming as perceived by the EU is no longer a craft, perfected over generations by a particular people to suit particular landscapes, adapted carefully to changing conditions and possibilities, rather it has become a physical translation of legislation operated upon the land. This legislation is put in place with many agendas, it is strongly influenced by

15

urban thinking and attitudes about rural places and seems to rely heavily on abstract thinking and science. (*see* the 'food' chapter, page 43).

leisure landscapes

This scientific approach to agriculture is uncomfortably married to a heritage agenda. This agenda legislates for a landscape where the historical agricultural livelihood of the rural inhabitants is to be replaced by a touristic one, where the few farmers remaining simply become guardians of a rural theme park, where inhabitants are unwelcome. These urban-based and Europe-wide diktats follow attitudes about the landscape that I recognize from my childhood, they seem to ignore the fact that the landscape in Ireland looks the way that it does because people live there and make their livelihoods there, it looks the way that it does because it was the site for the production of food and energy for this island. Instead, the landscape is understood as a picture postcard, a tourist resort that has to be preserved to be valuable, and the farmer is viewed as an innocent that needs directing. This is a nostalgic and conservative attitude and reduces the experience of the landscape and its occupants to the purely visual. It is a simplistic approach which forgets the function that the landscape has always had.

living landscapes

Our landscape is a complex system, constantly changing in response to a myriad of forces, formed by many hands over history. It is, above all else, a contemporary place where food can still be produced through physical work and careful husbandry. Rural population may well increase in response to labour needs to replace fuel use, or to opportunities afforded by communication technology, or they may decrease if food can be magicked out of elsewhere. What the future holds is impossible to foresee, what is possible is serious, rural-based thought which recognizes the landscape for what it is , a functioning place, which could, with careful planning, significantly contribute to the food and energy security of this island now and in the future, and be the site for a vibrant, healthy community.

The visual aspects of our landscapes are tied closely to what work is done there, the visual landscape changes as our farming practices change, as rural lifestyles alter. It is a functioning, changing place, not to be frozen into a picture postcard, nor a museum of bygone days.

MOBILE

Moses and the Mountain

Life in the countryside at the moment operates around fixed points. Roads have been improved to facilitate transport of the resources no longer available locally—the improving of roads and the distribution of cheap goods rendering the local production of resources redundant—and the people who have seen the ravages of years of rural depopulation have a natural instinct to move to more accessible places. Sites that are close to large roads are the most valuable. The closest towns are where the places of advertised entertainment are to be found alongwith places of work and education, therefore value is placed upon houses that although rural, surrounded by a little patch of controlled nature, a lawn, are within easy drive of these towns. The bigger the nearby town, the more possibilities for work and fun, the more valuable the house.

18

This peculiar state of affairs struck me from the start. Having decided to move to the country—we were thinking of green fields, the sound of birds singing, trees and a plot to grow some food—we kept being offered by every single estate agent overpriced minute fractions of acres deafened by the sound of passing cars. As we were looking to find somewhere to live (holiday houses could afford to feel remote) each prospective seller tried to play down the countryside aspect and brag about the access to nearby towns, motorways, etc. as if there could be no life without access to what we were in effect keen to leave behind.

In this way rural life has become suburban. We live now in a serviced landscape. Roads, rail (to a lesser degree), electricity, telephone, heating oil, food all have to be delivered to rural areas for life to carry on. The state has fully embraced rural Ireland, it is as serviced as urban areas, with a thorough infrastructure. Motorways, electricity pylons, mobile-phone masts, articulated lorries full of food and oil tankers criss cross the landscape bringing a new lifestyle to rural areas, there is no *beyond the pale* anymore, but at what cost ?

A lot of energy is put into moving people from one place to another as quickly as possible, very definitely from any spot in rural Ireland to Dublin (see the road and railway maps). Work and leisure are removed from the home, and the countryside is alive only with the sound of people driving around from place to place. This leads to a general belief that living in a rural house is in essence 'unsustainable', by which people mean that it is heavy in fossil-fuel use. This lifestyle also leads to a dissolution of a sense of community in rural areas which are now more often than not made up of houses occupied in the evenings only, by tired people watching television while worrying about their mortgage repayments.

The forms of economic and social development pursued throughout the latter half of this century have resulted in this situation, for it was not always so. The patterns of life in rural areas were quite different, and were built upon a much more economic use of movement.

Mobile Cinema
The year before last I attended a two-day festival of Werner Herzog films. It took place in a nearby small town, in a state-of-the-art hundred seat cinema. All kinds of people came down out of the mountains for the festival.

This was able to happen in a small town with no fixed cinema because Leitrim County Council, our local authority, invested in a mobile cinema. This cinema travels from town to town as an articulated lorry. It stops, plugs into the mains, and unfolds. Fifteen minutes later the town has a cinema… which you can walk to. Replacing in the smaller towns the cinemas that have long closed their doors.

It seems revolutionary that something as large as a cinema can move, but if we look in the past we see the mobile library and bank in the 1970s, and earlier still, shops, markets, fairs, circus, a whole world was on the move.

good neighbours
My neighbour George is, to borrow his phrase, 'the best of the best'. He is kind, gentle and extremely entertaining. Having worked as a bartender for most of his life and having a good ear for stories, he knows everybody for miles and has a good or at the very least amusing word to say about all. He rarely travels beyond Mohill, about 3 miles away, although once a year his sister-in-law may drag him away to Mayo for a day.

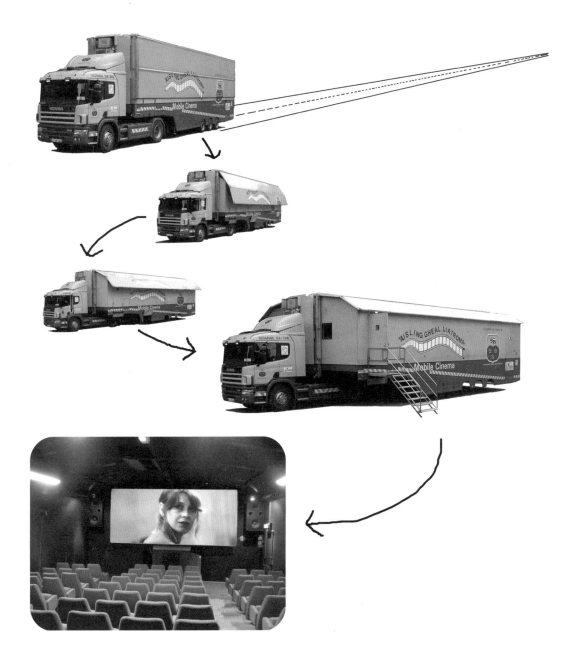

He grew up in the 1950s surrounded by many more people than live here now. In those days there were over thirty people living on our lane, now there are only six (including our family of four). On a day-to-day level more people brought more fun. Lots of conversations during the course of the working day, lots of asking for and receiving help for tasks requiring more hands, and in the evening music, card-games and stories around someone's fire. There were three mobile shops, Tommy Kelly with horse and cart, Bernie Quinn with a lorry, and Jack McBride with a tractor and trailer. It was a walk to the pub in the village of Cloone, about 25 minutes, and for a dance hall on a special night you had to get on a bike. Once a week there was a market in Mohill, it was one-and-a-half hour walk away or a cycle ride, but it was worth it, livestock and produce to sell, people to meet, and all kinds of journeying traders and musical types, all the stuff you did not have at home.

A few weeks ago McCormicks' circus came to Cloone community centre. It was quite amazing in that it consisted of just one family, two parents and their two sons aged 12 and 16. They put on a two-hour show on a Sunday afternoon, and by Monday lunch-time had packed up and headed to the next village. I got talking to George about this and he started to tell me about the circuses of his childhood. In the 1950s a circus would come to Mohill about twice a year, big ones, Duffy's and Fossett's being the notable ones that are still around today. He told me that all the men and children would have gone for a day into town. I looked into the history of the circus in Ireland to discover that in 1870, for example, Duffy's circus was on the road with two hundred and fifty horses with a one-mile street parade. As well as this in George's youth there were three big fairs a year in Mohill and two in Cloone, so all in all, to balance a day-to-day life of hard work there was great entertainment.

I can relate to this too, my parents went to live in England when they were married, and until I was four years old we lived in a village in Buckinghamshire, from which my father commuted to London. Just like George's stories once or twice a year the Circus came to the village. Sideshows, animals, clowns and strong men all appeared for a few days, and these constitute my first real memories so exciting it all seemed to me. The circus would pack up one morning and your heart would sink. Each time someone was rumoured to have ran off with the circus, some bored teenager looking for a life of freedom, who perhaps like me had their first memories of excitement at that circus and had left to become the assistant lion tamer, a new trapeze artist, or maybe just to travel to the next town.

What I find enlightening when George describes his life to me is that it seems rich through contact with people. There was enough diversity flowing through Mohill, travelling *to* him when home seemed boring. When he describes the circus his eyes light up with the memory of it with I believe quite a few more sparkles in his eyes than seen-it-all children who these days fly off to Disneyland or to Lapland to meet Santa describing their trips. George had really not wanted for anything except that as time went on, his neighbours and friends have died or moved away. We might dismiss that as too simple a life compared to our 'modern', 'sophisticated' existence, yet large gatherings of excited people is still what we are all after. The disappearance of people leaves our neighbour George more lonely than a natural socialite like him would like, but more importantly it means that the critical mass of people needed to support the travelling tradesmen and entertainers in fair towns like Mohill does no longer exist, so entertainment becomes television- and pub-based, or reliant on a car.

In contemporary terms he has a very small carbon footprint—he does not drive, he lives in the house that his father built using local materials, uses little electricity, as progress would have it, however, he had his solid-fuel range changed into an oil-fired one a few years back, but it's easy to understand as back then oil was cheap and was going to be forever and the local 'mud' turf is so poor and so work-intensive. His life's work in shops and as a barman has served the public, entertained them, given people company. When experts say that it is 'unsustainable to live in a one-off house in a rural area' I think of George and I laugh. The secret was the tradition of a mobility of services across rural Ireland.

travellers

The settled community looks at travellers at best with suspicion, more often than not as trouble-makers. Society traditionally mistrusts those who-do-not-do-as-we-do, and since the book of rules is written by the settled community a lot of effort is put into settling travellers, long-term in houses, or short-term in halting sites. This itinerant lifestyle is seen as a problem to be solved. This perceived problem might in fact be the solution to another problem : I believe that in fact the travellers may well be showing us one of the solutions to the current dysfunction of rural life—rather than creating a disruption. Travellers, Gypsies, Itinerants are the last stand of a large population of travelling tradesmen, journeymen and itinerant musicians, who have mended, built and made entertainment for rural people since the Middle Ages, and in living their lives on the move solved one of the intrinsic problems of rural life, the fact that a settled community can be a stifling thing, where conformity is required, where there is no place for new ideas.

It was not just entertainment that travelled, there used to be many travelling trades in Ireland, whitesmiths would travel door-to-door fixing pots and selling tools, weavers too and tailors, creel makers, all people who could not be supported by the work in any one district. Throughout Northern Europe the fair as a means of exchange and social intercourse is an institution far older than the town, and around Ireland some have survived—the Puck fair in August in Kerry, the horse fair in Ballinasloe are two that I know of, that last for a few days, but weekly fairs as a place to buy local foods and services are on the rise again around Ireland in the form of the farmers market.

markets

About two years ago a farmers market started in a nearby town. Mari-aymone set up a stall, *maison djeribi*, for which she bakes sourdough bread and French *pâtisseries*. This allows us to exchange bread for food from the other stalls and means that if we accept— apart from the dry staples that we order in bulk—to eat only organic seasonal produce we only enter the doors of a supermarket to buy butter and cream.

For me it is in the politics of food, its production, its sale and its consumption, that the small choices that we make have the largest impact on our lives, our local land- scapes and the environment as a whole.

The sale of food is simply the business of getting it from a farm onto your table while remunerating the farmer. Forty percent of freight on the roads is moving food hither and thither, and around the mass food industry lies an extraordinarily complex and expensive system of distribution that is only maintained by the buying power of the supermarket keeping prices paid to farmers uneconomically low. For example a head of cabbage for which a farmer received 40 cents may sit on a supermarket shelf with a €1.40 price tag. The divorcing of consumer from producer has meant that a mesmerizing array of food safety standards have had to be drafted and enforced, since trust is unable to happen at the global scale that supermarkets operate at.

A local market solves many logistical problems.

1. It is local, so the food does not have to travel very far. This means that the food we eat becomes less reliant on imported energy.
2. The person selling the food has produced it, he is a member of your community, if he makes a salami that is poisonous, he will simply lose his customers. This means that standards are self regulating. The farmer becomes a visible part of the food chain with direct responsibilities to his customer.
3. The farmer or producer gets a fair price for his food. This makes farming more attractive and profitable. More people can move back into farming, which means more people inhabiting the land and listening to birdsong.
4. The landscape becomes once more essential to the lives of the people that live in it as it is where the food comes from, it becomes more used, and cared for as a resource.
5. The consumer gets good value as the goods are not reliant on numerous middlemen making a profit.
6. Because the market happens only once a week there is an intensity of use that means a community of market users and traders grows up, shopping becomes a social thing, an event, an enjoyment, not a chore.

All this being accomplished not by a revolution, not by draconian planning laws, just by a change of shopping habits.

infrastructure

The mobility of services is the key to a functioning rural community. The growing farmers market movement is concerned mainly with food. What is hopeful, however, is the fact that a mobile structure, the farmers market, can service a rural area very effectively for its food needs and that we can look at this structure as the germination of a bigger idea, we can examine what else can be hung onto it. Historically the weekly fair sold food, but this aspect was of more interest to the gardenless town dweller, for the farmer the fair allowed him to exchange his goods for money which he could then use to buy services, equipment or entertainment that were not available locally. It was much more then than a food market.

This is where the potential for our growing system of farmers markets lie, add to the market the mobile cinema, bank and library, a computer expert, a doctor, and market day becomes full of opportunities for both trader and consumer, a day out, social contact and all close to home.

Society does not have the resources to service the rural landscape as if it were a spread-out city. We need to invent a new mobile infrastructure, that learns from the past and celebrates a different ethos, a dynamic future that draws on the most modern technology, yet fulfils the most ancient desires.

NATURAL ARTIFICIAL

the comfort of a dichotomy

The society that we live in has very clear ideas about what is natural and what is artificial. The word artificial is from the Latin *ars* 'art' and *facere* 'make', implicit in this is that it is man that does the making. Natural, as defined in the Concise Oxford Dictionary is something 'not made, caused by, or processed by humans'. We were all educated with this understanding of a division, whether science, architectural theory or environmentalism the world was always divided into two, the natural and the artificial.

One of the bases of our society is religion, and certainly Christianity is firm in the notion that God gave man dominion over the animals and over nature, that the universe centred on man. Environmentalism, for many a science, for others a new religion, similarly places man in the centre as custodians of nature, the ones responsible, the ones in charge. It seems that the rich and powerful have centred their science, culture and art on this sense of self-importance for as long as modern civilization has existed.

Architecture exists in this cultural construct as well, we always view the building as being something that sits on the landscape, separate to it both in definition and visually. When we look at a farmed hillside with a new house built in the middle of it we ask 'Does it fit in ?' 'Does it not spoil the view ?' There is 'the view', that is understood as nature, and 'the house', that is understood as an artificial addition.

animals

Keeping animals was an eye opener for me. I had never given much thought to how animals interact with their environment before, and it surprised me how much animals form where they live to suit their needs and feeding habits. Our ducks roam free range, however they chose the dampest place around our house and set to work on their mud-flat, wet-land landscaping project. What used to be grass is now muddy, puddly and wet, the ducks wander around rooting in the soft ground, drinking and generally doing all the things that ducks like to do while not swimming. So I learned that animals through their activities alter landscape just as we do, do they feel in control ? Do our goats, as they are chewing the cud, see themselves also at the centre of the universe ? Did the goat god give them dominion over us and make us provide food and shelter ?

Sciences have always supplied us with the proof that we are different, and over the years many different theories have existed to keep us neatly separated from nature. The most important was that man uses tools and animals do not. It was in Africa in the 1960s that Jane Goodall, a research scientist working with Louis Leakey, the anthropologist, first observed a chimpanzee using a stem of grass to extract termites from a nest. It caused scientific uproar, Louis Leakey responded to the news with the famous remark 'Ah! Now we must redefine man, redefine tool, or accept chimpanzees as human.'

termites, tool makers
Most creatures are extremely effective at making their environment comfortable, using limited means and this allows them to thrive.

There are a huge amount of termites in the world, it is estimated that there are five hundred kilograms of termites for every human alive, on a much tinier land area. They accomplish this density primarily because of the skillful architecture and engineering of the termite mounds. The termites of sub-Saharan Africa build mounds in mud which stand on average 3-metre high and contain a complex system of channels and ducts of different sizes. The termites do not live in these mounds, rather, their nest lies in the ground underneath it, the mound serves to regulate the temperature and humidity of the nest while ventilating it. Its exact size and design is continually modified to deal with changing populations and seasonal climatic differences.

Within the nest temperatures fluctuate no more than one degree Celsius while outside daytime temperature exceeds forty degrees and night-time plummets to below freezing. The million or so inhabitants produce collectively the same respiratory gas exchange as a cow, and this is also dealt with within the mound. They farm a fungus just above the nest, which is allowed to rot prior to eating to aid digestion. This is carried out with a minimum of energy, the construction and upkeep of a typical mound involves no more than 10 per cent of the colony's annual expenditures of energy.

In making such a perfectly tuned tool the termites have been able to externalize many bodily functions, particularly temperature control, digestion and respiration. This is done with no input of external energy apart from what is passively available on site. Thus their race is able to thrive with little environmental damage.

It seems that there is a lot that we can learn about the construction of environmentally stable structures from these mounds, and a multi-disciplinary team from Loughborough University in England is carrying out an amazing research project that is studying the mounds and trying to apply what they are discovering to the task of proposing more intelligent structures for human habitation.

This termite mound, in its extreme complexity of form, simplicity of material and functional effectiveness is a compelling object. It stands however as something ambiguous, for me it is an example of an artefact that does not rest happily in a natural classification, nor in an artificial one. It starts to question this classification system entirely.

structures in the landscape

If we look at it coldly, rationally, leaving religion and philosophy to the side, the building work done by animals is no different to that carried out by man, perhaps it is less concerned in general with aesthetics (though the bauer bird constructs monuments to attract a mate), the thing that often makes it stand out is its effectiveness with regard to survival within a given landscape, using limited means.

If we accept man as a part of the natural world it leaves us in a very different position when examining our houses and settlements, they become simply natural phenomena that are either effective for their use or not. We are just one of countless millions of interdependent living and inanimate systems that have a complex web of relationships with each other, and our survival as one of these systems depends on our ability to co-exist in a sensitive balance with the others.

All we really ask of our houses is that they keep us warm and dry, and protect us from intruders. At the moment we achieve this with huge wastage of energy and material. These simple demands should be obtainable through passive means utilizing only local materials in all but the least hospitable landscapes. Over the last century using fossil-fuel reserves have made us lazy in this regard, because in fact, like the houses of animals, our architectural heritage of vernacular buildings were simple, smart and easy to construct. If we learn from our past and from species around us and add to this our contemporary technical know-how and our intellectual cleverness as a species we can once more make houses that are a balanced part of the landscape in which they are sited as opposed to being hosted by that landscape.

buildings

The size of things is of fundamental importance. This is perhaps obvious at least certainly with regard to the function of objects. A spoon has to be able to fit in your mouth, a chair must be just the right height to be comfortable, a doorway high enough that you don't have to stoop on entry to avoid hitting your head. Lots of thought goes into this and hundreds of years of measuring, testing and the development of the science of ergonomics, has left us with an understanding of what in theory should feel right as long as you are *the average person*. We live in a *one size suits all world* which means nothing is quite right any more. In the past the rich had tailored made-to-measure clothes, and the poor had home-made made-to-measure clothes, now we exist in an impoverished approximation of comfort necessitated by mass production as opposed to craft.

Architects are also interested in scale, in size. The whole sense of a building is wrapped up in its scale, obviously its usefulness depends, just as it does for objects, on approximating its correct sizing, so the architect studies the steepness of stairs, the widths of corridors, the height of railings. Buildings are made to suit the movements of the human body, and in this the architect becomes choreographer of the dance of life where building transcends the functional and becomes a beautiful uplifting thing.

As I am writing this I am thinking of buildings by the architect Hans Scharoun. He made a series of public buildings in Berlin in the 1960s and early 70s, the most famous being the Philharmonie, a classical concert hall completed in 1963, and home to the Berlin Philharmonic Orchestra. In its foyer many people can gather, you are aware of people around you, groups and clusters. You move from foyer to auditorium with ease, a stairs always seems to present itself when needed, and then the gathering place, the auditorium which seats 2200 people seems intimate, you feel yourself close to the orchestra and not swamped by the other 2199 people around you.

In contrast to this, as a student, inter-railing around Europe one summer, I found myself in Milan central station. It is a scary building, suddenly I was an ant amongst a multitude of other ants. It is quite simply put, huge. Scaled for some race of giants, grandiose and bombastic, it dwarfs you, you seem insignificant, while its creators seem powerful and important. Never before had a building seemed so political to me, so expressive of a set of ideas about the relationship between the citizen and the state. It was designed by an architect called Stacchini, commissioned by Benito Mussolini, the fascist dictator, and was completed in 1931. Bombastic and grandiose it is a very successful design on its own terms, expressing fully the sense of state that existed in Italy at the time.

So the relationship between the scale of the human and the scale of a building can say a lot about the ideas or ideals of the society who built it, and the architect is the translator of these ideas or politics into built form which then affects deeply the life of the people who use the building.

landscape
The buildings that I mention above were built with the intention of emotionally affecting the people using them. Landscapes have a scale too which emotionally affect their occupants.

Ever since humankind has settled the land he has brought his scale to bear on landscapes, man has worked hard at domestication, endeavouring to make the landscape a comfortable, hospitable place to live, making countless interventions to bring his scale to bear, working with his body, working the ground, tending plants and trees, the landscape has been settled. Hedgerows and stone walls contain, protecting crops, animals and people from winds, houses nestle behind shelter belts of trees. Lazy beds are made, the scale of the shovel, turf cuttings the scale of the slane, paths to suit a barrow or cart. The landscape becomes slowly like a perfectly crafted tool that sits comfortably in the hand, everything the right scale, everything in the right place, everything suited to what goes on there. Just as I was thinking about Hans Scharoun's Philharmonie as I discussed buildings, here I am thinking about the landscape around a house I know in Co. Sligo, on the coast near Easkey. It is in a landscape that has been occupied constantly since neolithic times. Walking around the area about the house is extraordinary, it is easy, comfortable, paths are sheltered and dry, seats placed for the sun (though originally designed for the sun sterilizing of milking jugs), a magical, easy place.

This type of landscape has been formed over thousands of years in Ireland. It is a crafted thing that was made in response to the life lived in it, no grand ideas, just the necessity of survival through the power of men with shovels and barrows, through the needs and tastes of domesticated animals, it is an instinctive thing, a natural thing.

A landscape achieves this human scale when it is worked by a people on their own terms, responding to common sense, tradition, and serving their day-to-day needs. Throughout history there is another layer, another ordering device acting on the landscape, that of the state, landlord, or business.

the extraction of wealth

Government and businesses operate at a larger scale to the ordering devices of the personal landscape that I have described above, and they have different concerns. Primarily urban based, they see it as a resource : food for the urban table, rent for the landlords' pocket. The landscape must conform to an economic model of trade, growth, money and tax. The subsistence farmer contributes little to the greater economy, his life cyclical rather than progressive, no energy or money goes into his existence and none comes out, he has no part to play in a growth economy.

This scale of influence has existed since the time of organized society. In the Ireland of the seventeenth century the Tudor planters were particularly irritated by the easy-going wandering life of the Irish pastoralist and sought to anchor the nomadic natives to tillage farms where the more settled round of duties would tire them out and leave less time for 'mischief'.

In the eighteenth and nineteenth century throughout Ireland, though predominant in the West and other areas of marginal land, there existed a form of comparatively dense settlement system centred in small nucleated settlements called clachans and practicing a farming system referred to at the time as rundale. In rundale the land-holding was organized communally (frequently the identity of the holding has remained in the form of the townland divisions). The cluster of houses was surrounded with the best land which was called the infield, which was a large open field, without enclosures but divided into strips separated by sods or stones, here oats and potatoes and vegetables were cultivated. These strips were re-distributed every few years between families to ensure a fair division of the different qualities of soil present. The outer edge of the infield was delineated by a sturdy wall, and the area beyond that wall was the outfield which was treated as commonage where grazing was organized communally, each family being allowed a certain number of animals. This system grew up on landscapes that consisted of marginal bog or mountain lands that had a scattering of glacial drift of better soil quality. These became the infield which in its permanent cultivation drew on the non-arable commonage for a balanced nutrient flow in the form of manure (mostly from cows), sand, seaweed, peat or sods. This system represented an intelligent use of the ecological conditions to hand which maximized the carrying capacity of a meagre environment using a careful judgement of the balance between limited arable land and extensive marginal grazing land, and where money was scarce and labour plentiful.

The colonial state believed that only individual farms as existed in the English countryside would encourage initiative and self reliance, as opposed to the system of mutual aid present in Ireland through the rundale system. Aided by the potato famine of the 1840s they set about breaking up this communal existence and replacing it by individual holdings, the scattered settlement pattern that we see the remains of today, where each nuclear family has an independent holding with house on site. A good example of DIVIDE AND RULE.

Somehow through all these enforced changes the landscape retained its human scale, and through the density of these scattered houses a scale of community existed, despite external forces whose motivations were profit or order as opposed to care for the welfare of the rural inhabitant.

the scale of the modern landscape
The scale of the modern landscape is changing. It is being formed by machinery not people, in response to a scale of ordering, of policy never experienced before.

Central government makes policy for rural Ireland tailored not to suit its landscape, but tailored to suit the demands of the European Union, it is a one-size-fits-all approach to law making, and behind it is a belief in intensive farming that, as discussed elsewhere (*see* below, page 43, the 'food' chapter), is inappropriate for many Irish landscapes.

Since the 1970s farmers have been encouraged through grants and advice from bodies like Teagasc to intensify, to follow a productivist mode of farming. In physical terms this has produced a larger scaled landscape as hedgerows have been removed to make fields bigger, tracks wider and more suitable to the scale of the tractor or combine harvester. Smaller farms have been accumulated into bigger holdings. Larger sheds accommodate greater numbers of cattle, fed with meal from larger trucks. As farming becomes mechanized, there is less need for labour on the farm, so populations either reduce, devastating communities, or diversify, their work practices often involving commute times greater than a suburban average. As farming has specialized the local food market has disappeared so all food gets imported into rural shops, which are no longer local, rather they have become enormous sheds on the outskirts of towns. As services become bigger and more centralized the rural population becomes increasingly car dependent, roads become bigger. The scale has increased, no longer a place for man, rather a place for the car, the tractor, the lorry.

With energy prices on the increase this urban influenced rural existence is going to get more expensive and thus less possible. It will be more costly to farm if we are to continue on our fossil-fuel reliant intensive farming model, more expensive to import food, and to go out to buy it, more expensive to heat our homes. Servicing homes and people spread out and detached from each other will be well nigh impossible. Simply put, shipping energy into remote places is going to become a luxury that society cannot afford.

The model we are following has been put in place based on decisions and assumptions from afar. It is quite simply wrong, rural areas are not like dispersed cities, rural lifestyles cannot be urban, the scale of servicing a dispersed settlement pattern from central locations is inappropriate. We are all wearing the same ill-fitting mass-produced suit.

local decision making

Where the rundale system to me seems a sophisticated, careful and intelligent use of a landscape, our modern farming methods seem simplistic, and I believe the reason for this is the way in which each system came about. There was no big idea inherent in rundale, it just evolved. Evolution allows us to respond to complex situations, a system of millions of simple decisions are made over time which add together into a complex whole, which is recognizable as a natural system which works. This happens from the ground up, and is formed by the people on site who are carrying out a continuous process of action and reflection, any changes to the system have to be carefully considered as survival depends on not making mistakes. In contrast to this, modern farming is full of ideas based on theories developed by people not on site, acting from afar, and whose survival is in no way bound up in the success or failure of practice, and whose motivations are different and more often than not, simpler than those who will put the theory into practice. These farming techniques are developed without an interest in the specifics of each landscape relying instead on importing chemicals and machinery onto the farm, also from afar, turning the farmer into a consumer both of ideas and equipment.

We need to find a system of decision making that can happen at a local scale and in some way mimics the complexity of evolution and the diversity of place and situation. Today the greatest innovators in this area seem to be found in South America.

participatory democracy
Paulo Freire was a teacher working in the state education system in Brazil in the early 1960s. He developed literacy programs that were centred on people talking instead of the monologue of the teacher. He believed that he needed to focus teaching on the problems and realities faced by the illiterate poor, working with them in small groups he called *cultural circles*.

He centred learning on a discussion of the common experiences of the group, analysing local conditions, and developing projects to allow them to act on this reality. In concrete terms the work started with the twenty-five or so members of the *cultural circle* getting to know each other and their linguistic basis. In this first session *generative words* were selected, these were chosen to be both phonetically and socially rich. In the following session the organizer had prepared slides which represented the words in

40

pictures which were discussed in terms of their social and cultural meanings. After this the words were finally analysed in their written form, then divided into syllables which were recomposed by the group into new words.

Freire showed that it did not need more than 17 generative words to learn to read in about thirty hours in total. At a time in Brazil where only the literate could vote this was an intensely political program, and understood by Freire as such. These circles left the participants not just with the tools of literacy that allowed them to be part of political life, but also with a heightened sense of the society they lived in and an understanding of their ability to change their situation just as they had changed their reading and writing skills. When the right-wing government was formed in 1964 following a *coup*, Freire was imprisoned and then exiled. He continued his work abroad, and returned to Brazil in 1979 where he helped create the Brazilian Workers Party and form its ideas on participatory democracy utilizing his *cultural circles* model.

These ideas on participatory democracy have found their most extensive use in Venezuela where there is at present a strong commitment to the creation of a participative, social state to replace the centralized, bureaucratic state in existence. Communal councils are being set up to represent each community of about 200 families in an urban environment, about 20 families in the countryside. Through this the community becomes the basic structural unit of government. Experience shows that in small groupings people are more able to exercise their power to analyse their needs and priorities, and to put in place projects and structures that are to the benefit of the communities. Planning, health, educational, agricultural, all kinds of projects are being conceived, developed and organized by the local community, funded by the government. Discussing, debating, executing and supervizing projects that solve local problems and take local opportunities give a community real power. It means that while organizing and carrying out development projects people learn how to act together in society, how to realize their potential, and through an understanding of these micro systems they gain an understanding of larger systems of power and control.

structures in rural ireland

The basic geographical unit of rural Ireland is the townland, which in a lot of cases was the area of land farmed by a single clachan under the rundale system. These are collected together to form a parish by the Catholic Church which is normally similar to an electoral area. Most parts of local life are organized at the scale of the parish. I live in the sparsely populated townland of Annaghmaconway (population of about 16) which is in the parish of Cloone (population about 327). The organizations that operate at the scale of the parish include a GAA club, a community centre with various activities, a guild of the Irish Countrywomen Association, a number of separate water schemes and a neighbourhood watch organization. These peripheral organizations do serve to bind people together and give them a collective identity, and are valuable for that.

It is at this scale, perhaps formed of representatives from a townland scale that rural Ireland might work best, where people might find a voice, and feel connected with both people in their locality and to the structures of power. It is at this scale that a knowledge of a craft of how to live in a particular landscape exists, and it is at this scale that people can remember and relearn the pleasures of helping each other, relying on one other, of a communality that existed in our past and will be essential for our future.

The thinking about rural Ireland, about its agriculture and settlement patterns, must happen at a smaller scale, a local scale specific to particular landscapes. It must put in place local policies that can respond to change in fossil-fuel prices and availability, and nurture a structure that facilitates good community building *what is going on ?*

Food is one of the most important things in my life. Really, when I look at it, shelter, food, company, that is what it all comes down to, if you get these right you have more than enough for a great life.

In the 1990s minimalist architecture was all the rage. The thing that marks this stripped down, seemingly simple architecture for me is how complicated it is to achieve. Behind the scenes is a technical nightmare, a complexity that always has to remain hidden for the project to look right, a complexity that is expensive. I am more drawn to things that are simple in their essence. So it is with food.

It seems so simple, you just go into a big supermarket and it is all there for you to buy, but if you start examining the story of how the food on the shelves was produced and distributed you start to realize what the costs of this seemingly simple shopping style are.

From intensive farming, to trade agreements and production subsidies to complex distribution, nothing is what it seems. The farmer is unhappy, subsidized yet still underpaid, the food is none too fresh. In a world where half the population live in rural areas and a large proportion of these people are farmers, the livelihood of farmers is important. We all eat food, and we all live quite close to farms where food is produced ; why have the mechanisms of food distribution become so complex ?

the vernacular

Up until the twentieth century the survival of cities had always depended on its agricultural hinterland serving up its food requirements. Control of this hinterland was therefore necessary to ensure a good affordable food supply, and so rural areas would normally have been governed by one city or another. Rural areas were made up of this governed, productive area, and of the more remote wilderness areas, good for hunting, subsistence or nomadic farming, but not economically valuable. In Europe, these wilderness areas have all but disappeared as the food needs of the industrial revolution population growth were met by expansion of the area of farmed land. The method of farming remained pretty constant over this time and up until the second world war the life and work of the farmer on a day-to-day basis had been the same for centuries.

the modern movement

After the second world war a number of forces came to bear in Europe on what was still essentially a craft activity. The price of food became a political instrument. Reducing the cost of food was used as a technique to cut living costs, and therefore to keep potential wage increases to a minimum. With the EU Common Agricultural Policy farmers began to be paid subsidies so that their produce could be sold cheaper, often below the cost of production. We expect now to pay much less for food, 1 kg of round steak can cost a mere €8.67, now, compared to (inflation corrected) a whopping €15.20 in 1973. Farmers in Ireland now receive less than a quarter of the final selling price of their produce, the rest going on transport, distribution costs and the profits of others. Food, the main production of rural areas, is worth much less that it was, yet we are surprised that it is difficult to make a living through farming ?

At the same time, the channels of food distribution have become increasingly complex. This reached such a point that in the 1990s a journalist in England tracked meat going through 30 hands between farm and consumer (one hopes they were all washed!), more middle men, each having to make a living, selling a product that is getting cheaper and cheaper. The growing supermarket sector controls this distribution network, and uses its scale to control buying prices from the farm, and therefore reduce selling prices to the consumer.

The third factor was the growth during the second world war of the explosives and chemical industries. At the end of the war these industries had no market for their products. They had to find one. Intensive farming manages its intensity through the importation onto the land of fertility in the form of nitrogen. Nitrogen traditionally gets 'fixed' into land by plants such as clover that take nitrogen from the air, store it, and are then either eaten by livestock whose dung is used as fertilizer, or it is simply ploughed back into the ground with its precious nitrogen to nourish the ground. Nitrates are the basic constituent of explosives, but spread on the land serve to fertilize it in the short term. When farming intensively the other factor to deal with is pest control. The development of chemical warfare produced the answer to this problem. Chemical warfare technology adapted to making weed killers and pesticides. Nitrates and pesticides have become significant sources of pollution, the by-product of intensive farming.

So, using the short-term shortcuts of intensification through fertilizer and pesticide use and by utilizing cheap energy in the form of oil, cheaper food could be produced and moved from farm to shop more cheaply, to feed the hungry city dwellers

As the sweep of global trade increased and food from other countries with lower wages arrived on the scene, governments continued their cheap food policy using more and more subsidies, and this has now been accepted as the norm. Society has gone from viewing the farmer as supplier of nourishment from a healthy countryside, to a costly nuisance, who, while being propped up with subsidies, is reaping environmental havoc, and producing potentially poisonous food.

emerging movements

Luckily, farming has centuries of history to fall back on. The experiment of the last fifty years, instigated by politics and the greed of the middleman can be seen to have failed. It is generally accepted that energy prices are set to rise and this alone (without even taking into account the problems that such farming causes) must force a re-evaluation of our farming and food-distribution techniques, which are fossil-fuel reliant.

energy

Ireland exports 93 per cent of its beef production, so money is made on exports. However, the more intensively these animals are raised, the more energy is used, and this energy is imported, so in simple terms, the more oil goes up in price, the more expensive and uncompetitive Irish beef becomes.

Since roughly speaking we raise beef—using energy—to buy energy, could we simply not use a portion of our agricultural land to generate energy and therefore be less dependent on the fluctuations of the international beef and energy markets ? Common sense may have gone amiss at some stage in our developemnt.

local

Since the farmer is only getting a quarter of the value of his produce into his hand, if he changes the way that his food is sold, he could make much more money, even when you factor in processing costs. Farmers markets (*see* pp.25–6) are springing up all over the country, and, as was the case fifty years ago, you can buy all your food there, fresh, local and from someone who is able to make a living without 'handouts', and with considerably more pride in his/her trade.

KEARNS GROWERS

Catherine and Rosaleen Kearns run an organic vegetable garden in Rooskey in county Roscommon and sell their produce at a number of farmers markets around them.

The land that they farm is where they grew up. Their father grew vegetables all his life for a living, travelling to the local towns a few times a week to deliver to grocery shops. This was a precarious existence, reliant on year-to-year success, but it saved him from working at the local meat factory, even though he had just two and a half acres of land. He grew vegetables on about two acres and kept about five cows on the remaining land from which he collected manure to fertilize his garden. Catherine remembers having to always graze the cows up and down the edges of roads to keep them fed. Their garden lies on marginal ground which through the life-long work and knowledge

47

of their father now has good quality top-soil. They remember his amazing instinct, being able to look at the plants and the soil and know exactly what they were deficient in, what nutrients they needed. Catherine explains it as being a much more intimate relationship with the ground than people have now, where the soil test reigns, and the experts analysis guides what is done.

The two daughters married and both reared families who have now left home. Three years ago, after many years of talking, thinking and dreaming about it they took over their father's garden which had got smaller and smaller as he got older.

They grow vegetables outside and in polytunnels : leeks, potatoes, carrots, salads of all varieties, peas and beans, cabbage, turnips, cabbages, courgettes, cucumbers, beetroot, spinach, chard, onions, radishes, scallions, cauliflower and brocolli, and also fruit, raspberries, strawberries, blackcurrants, redcurrants and gooseberries. Rosaleen and her husband have 30 acres of land and they keep 9 cows which keeps them supplied with incoming fertility in the form of manure.

They work very hard, in effect all the hours of daylight both winter and summer. In the summer they start early, about 5.30 am, though they rest during the early afternoon when the sun is really hot. The two of them are there every day almost except when they are at farmers markets three mornings a week, and their husbands help when they can, especially in the summer when things get very busy. They are confident that they can make a living at it, which will become even more important when Catherine's husband Dennie will lose his job when the local meat factory closes next year.

EDEN HERBS

Rod Alston set up Eden Herbs with his then partner Dolores Keegan in 1977. He grows fruit, vegetables and herbs. He has run it on his own since 1992. They have always had a mixture of students, apprentices, casual workers or wwoofers (willing workers on organic farms) working alongside them especially in the summer. He has 21 acres in total, using 2 of them for horticulture, on some of the rest he used to keep 4 cows and some goats, now he just has goats and rents the remainder to a neighbour. On the remaining acres he has planted some mixed forestry.

He supplies local shops and restaurants with his produce, delivering twice a week and has always made a living from his work, grossing at the moment about €35,000 a year from his sales. He admits that he has simple habits and a deep psychological aversion to money, and like most farmers the distinction between work and leisure are blurred. He keeps a check on himself that he makes enough time in his life for the people around him that he cares about, and for playing music, which he does to great acclaim around Sligo. Like the Kearns, he works very hard—all the hours of daylight all year round—but he says he loves it, it is what he has chosen to do. The winter months spent tidying and preparing are tough and all that keeps you going is knowing what it will be like in June. But then June comes and it is like magic (*see* overleaf).

a new landscape
What is interesting in both of the above accounts is both the productivity and employment levels per acre of this type of farming compared to what is now usual in Ireland. Both operate with one person per acre of growing area in terms of labour, and get enough of a return to earn a living. Catherine's says that her father estimated that a quarter of an acre would feed a family, including a cow. This would mean that from one acre you are feeding four families, with the work of one person, say sixty hours per week, this would mean fifteen hours per family, about two days work a week.

This system of farming is tight in the present climate where low economic value is placed on food. However, if we instead evaluate time input, and understand a lot of what people now do as leisure, sport, workouts and walking can be replaced by more productive activities, food becomes cheap in relation to time input and the amount of land needed. To calculate land use areas, if we use Kearns growers as an example from which to extrapolate.

They have	30 acres pasture (grass)
	2 acres fruit and vegetables.
	2 people working
That is	94 per cent of land in pasture,
with the remaining	6 per cent with fruit and vegetables.
at the moment Ireland has	4.0 million hectares used as pasture
using our model then	3.76 million hectares remain as pasture
and	240,000 hectares fruit and vegetables.
with 2 people per 32 acres	600,000 people farming
compare	130,000 employed in farming at present
	65,000 processing and marketing
	195,000 total

That means three times as many people gaining a livelihood from farming, while catering for an increased consumption of fruit and vegetables which, given that Ireland had one of the lowest fruit and vegetable consumption per head in a recent European survey (well below the recommended 5-a-day), must be a good thing.

Using their father's estimate of 1/4 acre of growing area to feed a family, and adding the right proportion of pasture for fertility, we would have one family per about 3 hectares (about 7 acres). In basic terms the Irish population of 5,000,000 people (say 1,000,000 families of five) would need about 3 million hectares of farm land for vegetable and fruit food needs, which includes beef production at 94 per cent of current levels.

In terms of income in the present system, and using Rod Alston as an example :

Rod Alston makes €3,000 per acre of land per year minus costs (including his 5 acres for meat and manure production)

A farmer raising suckler cows on similar land makes profits of
€909
of which 75 per cent is made up of direct payments from the EU

which means €225 per acre profit in real terms.

I am not an agricultural economist, in fact I am not even an economist, but by working from these existing examples (two amongst many that I know) where I know that the people involved are making a living and, more importantly, have a fulfiling life, it seems that new models for agriculture can be introduced. By using local markets and home production to simplify distribution, and returning to a system which balances horticulture with meat production, in the way that rundale did in the past, an increased rural population will have access to good local seasonal food.

the vernacular

As I was studying architecture I met vernacular architecture in two places, in our own country in the past, and in other 'less developed countries' today. It seemed to belong to the historian or archeologist and the development architect overseas working with indigenous peoples—definitely not part of (my) contemporary life. The houses that I was interested in were all designed by architects and built by builders. They were commodities before they became homes. In practice you come across the word vernacular when planners tell you a house that you are designing should 'be in a vernacular style'. Is vernacular a style ? I rather think that it is a way of being, a *modus operandi*.

I often wonder what inspired us to go and build our own house, what made us think that we could do that ? On my part, I think that the confidence to do it came from two sources. in Berlin I spent a lot of time in squats where people took over and renovated old buildings to their personal and sometimes quite extreme tastes, doing the work themselves using salvaged material in buildings which for one reason or another nobody owned, or nobody was interested in. The other source was a small house self-built by the English architect Edward Cullinan in California in the 1960s with the aid of some students. This house was perhaps influenced by the work of Walter Segal, and I became interested in his approach to self building houses. His system of timber-framed houses that can be built by amateurs has survived for forty years, and it is with his basic system, upgraded to suit modern building regulations and our tastes that we built our own house. We seemed to have fallen into this world of the sixties, photos of men with ponytails and woolly side-burns, women with flowing dresses, bra-less, amazonian… I wondered whether we had become hippies.

We started to build in June 1999 and as we met the neighbours who were all offering us help in one way or another, I realized something extremely important. They had also all built their own houses, or at least helped their parents in the task. We were not hippies, we were in fact like everybody else around us.

What happens when you build your own house ?

1. It happens slowly. We lived in tents for a summer as we were building, this allowed us time to get to know the site in a more intimate way and therefore make better decisions with regard to positions of windows, doors, potentials for passive-solar gain.
2. Your neighbours get to know you slowly, they can help you, particularly as it is so much work they almost feel obliged to help, they feel a bit sorry for you. Padraig

56

Kelly, the man who sold us our site, and is now one of our neighbours was unbelievably helpful as we were building, first with advice as to where to get things and who to talk to, and then, as we got to know him more, he was up most weekends offering help with his son Dermot. I remember one day Padraig tossed eighty rolls of grass sods onto our roof to save us from hiring a lifting device. You become in this way indebted to them, and in many ways that is at the core of a community, people who know that they can rely on the help of others around them in times of need.

3. You become master of your house, it holds no secrets, a thing that you understand, that you can fix without calling in the experts. We live today with enough impenetrable machines that either get thrown out when broken, or fixed by specialists. The house should not be another of these, you should feel at home there, and as with people, you feel comfortable with those that you understand.

4. You live outside while building, so the whole site feels like your home. When later you are warm and snug in your house outside doesn't feel so dangerous, foreign. I remember the first night we took our bedding and slept in the house, yet it was much later that we started to cook and eat inside. We occupied the house in stages, 'When did you move in ?' is a question I cannot answer.

5. You don't owe the bank masses of money. I am interested in houses that are people's homes, not a commodity, not a 'step on the ladder', not part of that GNP producing merry-go-round that ties that house owner to twenty-five years hard labour. Instead of the worry of a mortgage you have aching muscles and a flush of pride.

6. It is never finished. A house is a process, not a product, we alter our house to suit our changing needs, it is an adaptable living thing.

learning by doing, learning from the past

It is only by doing things and then reflecting on your actions that you really learn, and by building our own home there were many lessons to learn. For me as an architect I for the first time felt myself inside the knowledge of building, how a building is constructed became more instinctive, less a learned discipline. More than anything it made me question the system under which our society constructs its houses. In getting a mortgage, what you are really doing is selling your confidence to a bank, you are saying 'I am confident that I will be able to pay you all this money over 25 years' the bank takes this, invents the money to give you (it did not exist until you asked for it) and charges you some more. The bank gets richer by charging you interest, the state gets richer in taxing the banks profits and the profits of the building contractor who builds your house and you are tied to staying in constant employment for the next quarter century, worried about keeping your job, you become a wage slave. My instinct had questioned this, but it was only by actually doing something that I could find alternatives.

The community that I moved into had a history of building their houses without too much debt, using the power of community and a knowledge of ways of building, however when something is so familiar you tend to forget its merits and now barraged by slick marketing by banks and building societies everyone who wants a house around me now are queuing up to sell their futures for the housing type seen on television, the ubiquitous suburban model.

People around me had been doing it in the past, I was doing it now, were other people also building their own houses ?

collecting

I love the blues, some of my favourite songs were 'collected' early this century by enthusiasts like Moses Asche travelling around the Mississippi delta with a tape recorder. When mari-aymone and I were commissioned by The Dock in Carrick-on-Shannon, to make an installation on architecture, we decided to focus on rural housing and talked to people and toured around rural Ireland in order to 'collect' examples of people who had built their own houses, hearing the reasons why they had done it, how it had gone, what it had done for their lives. I suppose we wanted to prove that the vernacular tradition is alive and well and down a boreen near you, that it is not a style that you can make a pastiche of, that it is a robust, pragmatic tradition.

Heleen moved to this site first in the early 1970s, she had a small child, a damp cottage, it was not a winter that she remembers fondly. She returned years later. She built this polytunnel house with Simon and carries on what might be described as the boolying tradition, they live in Holland for the winter months (October to February), and in Ireland for the other seven months. They make these two trips on bicycle and ferry, each trip an adventure, a journey of transition from one world to the other.

The house was cheap, probably around 2000 euros, and in it they live as they might in the Garden of Eden. All their food is grown there, their day is spent tending their garden/house, reading and writing. Inside, outside, living in a very simple way. There is no electricity, no running water, though a simple solar collector heats water for a shower. Lap-top batteries are charged ten minutes away at a neighbour's and twice a week e-mails checked in the local town, contact with the world at large. A network of friends live within cycling distance, so hard work can be measured against partying and chat.

Hugo and Ageeth bought this site with an existing barn in it, they are slowly building a new house on it, in the meantime they have converted a portion of the barn into a house. The primary intervention was a south-facing sun space with a deep concrete passive-solar heat collector. They insulated the barn to keep the heat in, and with the passive-solar gain from the sun room it is easy to heat the house with a small woodburning stove. The house sits in a tended, productive garden, and is connected to a large workshop.

63

Tom built this thatched house twenty years ago. Having spent a few years staying in other people's houses and renting houses around Leitrim and Roscommon he acquired a knowledge of the specifics of the local climate and a sense of the kind of house that he would like to live in. He had worked previously with a thatcher and had picked up enough to build a simple roof himself, so he decided to build a house that is more occupied roof than house to suit his skills. He keeps bees and farms a bit. Since his house cost him little he has been able to choose to do as he pleases and take time with his friends and neighbours. His grown up son has recently converted one of the outhouses to live in, giving himself a bit more privacy, yet remaining close to his dad.

new vernacular

Many of the people that we met were operating in the way that they did because they were on the margins of society, perhaps not able to get mortgages, not wanting to live in council accommodation. They had been forced to make houses themselves, yet through this they had forged a lifestyle in which they found immense satisfaction and empowerment. What seemed to be a disadvantage in fact had turned out to be a power of good. The vernacular is a way of doing things, not a visual style, it is very present in the Irish landscape. New vernacular buildings are, however, mostly hidden from view. Down backroads in cleverly sited houses, a multitude of people are quietly turning house owning into a joy, a freedom.

fatherhood

I moved to the countryside at much the same time that I became a father. Ezekiel, my son, was born when our house was enclosed, dry, if not warm, very rough and ready. Mari-aymone's work as an artist and publisher was as important to her as my work as an architect was to me and she pushed hard for sharing our parenting 50-50. I am eternally grateful to her for this as it opened up a whole new phase of my life. It seemed fair, but truthfully, I worried how it would impact on *my* work that always seemed demanding and important. It did indeed impact on my work, and my life, but in a hugely positive way by redefining the role of different kinds of work and activities in my life, and how one feeds into another.

The work practices that I was used to, that I had grown up with, and that predominate in our urban society were born of the Industrial Revolution.

The effect of the Industrial Revolution on Work and Family
1. Work became 'a job', a large number of workers gathered in one place to do highly coordinated tasks paced by machines, employed by a *boss*.
2. Workplaces grew to suit centralized manufacturing, big companies emerged in response to these economies of scale.
3. Centralized cities and later suburbs developed to suit big companies employing lots of workers, draining people from the countryside.
4. Mass marketing (selling the urban and later the suburban dream) used mass media to sell mass-produced products and lifestyles to the working masses, and their potential rural reinforcements.
5. At the end of each week, each worker got his own wage, for his own work, and brought it home to his family. Collectivism or mutual aid in work became non-existent.
6. The hierarchization of work already present was greatly increased, 'feminine' unpaid work was undervalued to such an extent that even when women rejoined the workforce they would be paid far less than men for equal work.
7. At the same time as growing unemployment—machines aiming to make people redundant—a cult of work, productive activity, was introduced, the only way to be valued in society was through brought-home pay.

Just as it affected work, the industrial revolution changed the face of family too.
1. A man became measured by his ability to support his family, it was his only concern. His ability to look after his children, and be a present husband was diminished.
2. Due to a lack of time he became either a disciplinarian 'wait till your father gets home' or an audience 'show daddy what you did today'.

3. Work and leisure became separated, each occupying fixed times and places. Home became the site of relaxation.
4. Children could not see or understand what their father did at work all day, further removing him from their lives and denying them the opportunity to understand the world of grown-ups.

rural work

Moving to Leitrim at the same time as becoming a father was serendipitous : The industrial revolution had affected rural Ireland perhaps less than anywhere else in Europe, leaving its occupants with very different work habits and lifestyle than their urban counterparts, and served as an example and support to our ideas about constructing our own balance of activities.

The Irish farming population in effect works from home as the house for the most part sits on the land that is farmed, and it has pretty much always been so. The whole day is made up of many different tasks, many requiring the help of other members of the family, spouse, children and also sometimes neighbours. Fathers who farm are around the house more, and the work they do is visible, as my neighbour George says of his childhood *everything we got came from the ground*.

Statistically now about a half of Irish farmers or their spouses have an off-farm job, and I see this also around me, leading to another change in structures as it is often the wife working, so more becomes is expected of the husband within the home.

To suddenly land in this world that wasn't structured in the usual work/home, man/woman divide was liberating, giving us further licence to really decide how we were going to parent and run our life, incorporating the way that we had both always dealt with our work, working for ourselves, enjoying our work, keeping odd hours. We were now surrounded by people who all had an array of activities and could not ever be defined by the one single focused profession that is expected from ambitious urban types. We were building a house and beginning to farm our five acres of land and I soon began to enjoy the mix of activities in the week—working in my office, doing site visits, looking after children, building and farming. We were living this balance between the intellectual, the physical and the caring sides of our make-up, and this was indeed replacing my envisaged life of hard work in the office, with recovery time at home with the family.

new work tendencies
How people work in rural areas is a little closer to our dominant historical experience as a species, people lived somewhere where they knew everyone and where people either worked alone or as part of a small focused team, for example a hunting trip or a meitheal. When you look at projections about how the internet may change our work habits you see similar tendencies. Technology has begun to change the structure of many companies, where smaller virtual companies can be made up of different teams working in different locations, using collaboration software. This could be people working from their own home, or gathered together in highly serviced community facilities. There is a flexibility of who you work with and where, allowing you to tailor your job to suit the situation, and also to suit other commitments. The way things are sold is also changing. Instead of large shops hoping to cater for everyone's tastes, things begin to specialize, a good example of this is Amazon, where 57 per cent of book sales are books that sell so little that you would never find them on the shelves of a normal sized bookshop.

part of a trend

The internet allows us to geographically disperse again, to move out of cities while still being productive in traditionally urban activities. My clients for the last years have almost exclusively been people moving out of cities to the countryside, while continuing to do the same jobs as before.

An example of this move my clients were making was the *inbetween house* which I completed in 2003. It was for the same family that I built my first job on returning to Dublin in 1995. At that time they had just bought a house in Ranelagh, close to Dublin city centre, and I designed for them a kitchen extension. The house had no garden, difficult parking on grid-locked streets, and they had two small children. They realized that there was no reason for them to be living in Dublin. Both are translators and their clients are in Germany, Switzerland and Italy for the most part, so long as they had an e-mail address and a telephone they could be anywhere. Now they live overlooking a beautiful lake, their children can walk to the local school, they work from home and have lots of land to grow food if they so wish. This pattern in the type of work that I am doing has continued, and I have either built houses for or got to know many people who are moving out of cities, working from home, not commuting and dramatically increasing their quality of life. This move brings new families to areas of depleted populations, brings diversity, and just as we have, allows the incomers to become part of a community which has an understanding of work that suits contemporary work practices.

As the world of work is redefined, opportunities to work from rural areas seem to increase, and when this is coupled to the fact that less income needs to be generated due to a relearned ability to make houses without falling into debt, the new rural dweller can diversify and find time to grow food or energy crops for their own or for the use of an expanded local population.

The structure of work patterns has moved away from centralized production in the immense factory, away from the moving of paper up and down the corridors of large office buildings.

There is an opportunity for society to learn from other patterns of work that are still practiced in rural areas, that suit a more balanced range of daily occupations, and that utilize the opportunities afforded us by the internet.

tents and caves

As an architect I enjoy reducing things to their essence, to try and understand them, to give them a clarity. Different buildings have different natures that arise through the material that they are made of and from the temperament of the people that built them. As I became more aware of the buildings around me this is what fascinated me the most, the building as a physical trace of a set of values, or of a lifestyle.

When we examine the history of architecture we have two strands, we have the tent makers and the cave dwellers.

The tent makers are assemblers, gathering an assortment of materials, understanding their strength and weaknesses, and joining them to provide shelter. Skins become covers, timber becomes structure, fibres become rope. These structures are in their nature light and transportable, they are the buildings of nomads.

73

All framed structures belong to this lineage, the pitched roof of our traditional houses, the steel-framed skyscraper.

The cave dwellers are excavators, burrowers, movers of earth, people who are of the earth. They form walls of mud, temples of stone, strong permanent fixed things which take enormous amounts of physical work, and achieve a strength through their mass and permanence. Their structures envelop and protect, they ground you. These are the brick walls, the concrete floors, the stuff that we cling to when we feel threatened.

symbiosis

Most contemporary buildings have a mixture of these two traditions, and in the architecture that I make I find it important to be aware of what piece relates to what tradition. When I look back over sketches and study models I can see that as a design develops I often make diagrams dividing earthwork from framework, I experiment with different functions in the different pieces. Thus in the mimetic house (*see* page 111) there is the buried, protected bedrooms with a framed living space above—freer, exposed, looking over the surrounding landscape, and in our own house, the framed pieces are anchored to a heavy earthbound wall of smaller intimate spaces.

achieving weight

With our own house we started with the framed pieces, they seemed easier to achieve. They use less material and less labour to enclose more space. I accepted this, and we began construction. With little groundworks to do, work really was quick, all hammers and nails, screwdrivers, and drills. It suited us and our type, people who grew up with little understanding of heavy physical work, its slow pace, its aching joints. When you make a frame, its strength, and your confidence in it relies on the design of the joints, the strength of the assemblage, you are trusting in something a little bit abstract, something that is strong enough but designed not be wasteful of effort or material. On windy nights I often wonder 'will it hold ?', I feel it is being tested. I feel it as a thing based on our intelligence—and that of the engineer—and that it relies on my confidence in it for its survival.

Mari-aymone's mother comes from Tunisia, and from her she has inherited a love for the earth buildings of that region. Thick walls, niches, a strong sense of containment. These are things that she could believe in more than a timber frame, our house had to have that sense to her. The heavy earthbound wall in our house was intended to be of rammed-earth construction. This seemed to us an elegant way of building : the use of a free resource, available all around us. Furthermore it drew on local vernacular house construction which in our landscape of drumlins and water, with a remarkable absence of stone, was almost entirely made of earth walls, save in the better houses where the colder northerly aspect was constructed of stone, if at all possible. Somehow it tied us to our new locality, this sharing of North African and Leitrim building techniques

I carried out a lot of research into clay types, mixes, formwork construction, but somehow it never seemed possible, even though our neighbours had all been doing it for centuries. Why ?

We were doing the building ourselves, as much as possible without the use of heavy machinery, which is expensive to hire, unpleasant to use and runs on fossil fuel. This meant that having a digger to mix the earth to the right consistency and place it in the formwork, was not an option. We would have been left, as people have been throughout history, with a very labour-intensive job, completely unfeasible in terms of our time.

This was why in the end we built these thick walls of strawbale, which was quicker, lighter and more insulating.

energy costs vs labour costs
The balance between the cost of energy and the cost of time is fundamental to how a society functions, and what the physical traces left by that society look like or consist of. In North and West Africa, where earth buildings are still built, there is an abundance of cheap labour, it is an economically poor society where people's time is cheap when compared to the price of oil. In Ireland where wages are high in comparison to the price of oil the opposite is true, time is expensive, material and transport cheap. This means at the moment in Ireland there is no economic advantage to using local material as transport is cheap, and speed of construction is important since wages are high. This has, as it has throughout the Western world, destroyed the tradition of craft (too time consuming) and removed all dignity from hand work. Most physical work in our society is now referred to as *unskilled labour*, a misnomer as anyone who has tried to yield a shovel will know…

Just as we all know that everybody needs exercise, that we must balance the physical with the mental in order to be healthy, so the same is true in society. Traditionally farming was the primary rural occupation, a physical occupation. There was no great stigma about being a farmer, it was hard work, but satisfying and with luck secure as you were producing food, one of society's necessities. Nowadays the measure used to evaluate how *developed* a country is, is in the proportion of the workforce involved in agriculture, the lower the better, so by definition the farmer is an *undeveloped* species, in need of modernization, of development. This situation can only exist because rich developed countries are able to buy food from poorer nations cheaply or subsidize their own produce. What little agriculture does happen in rich societies in mechanized so therefore not so labour intensive, but oil dependent.

A traditionally rural, agricultural country like Ireland suffers from this situation. What we value in our history is not valued and we must redefine what we are if we are to succeed in the modern world, but at what cost ? Can a society change so radically, so quickly ?

the future

Luckily help is at hand for those who value time over money. The energy-cost vs. labour-cost balance is a volatile equation, and we are in a period of history that will be marked by the rapid increase of oil prices as stocks become depleted. We, in the *developed* world will need to start examining the structures of our society in the past, and those of other countries that have remained less oil dependent. We will need to value local agriculture again as the only possible source of our food and energy, and value our return to a balance of the physical to the intellectual.

NETWORK

energy

Most convincing analysis of energy structures in the future depend on a networking of electricity supply and demand. At present electricity is generated in huge power stations, hubs, and then travels large distances to the site of the consumer. A complex infrastructure is necessary, and huge energy losses occur *en route*. The networked model is different. It proposes that every household and business become energy generators on a small scale and these all feed into the grid at times of over supply. Thus energy does not travel large distances so does not experience losses, and heat, which is the by-product of electricity generation can be used effectively instead of wasted.

This model for organization appeals to me, it always seems the most natural. As with a lot of the things that I have discussed in this book it puts the power, and the responsibility back in the hands of everyone, and at the same time cuts down on needless transport.

Around where I live, and I think across rural Ireland, children used to go to school with a lump of turf, or a few sticks in their pocket. With everyone's contribution, and an open fire, or pot-bellied stove, the schoolroom was warm for the day, when one pupil came empty handed it didn't matter so much, though a clip around the ear was probably administered. This is an example of a networked system, it is flexible across different sized groupings : more children in a bigger room means more turf and therefore enough heat, heat becomes the responsibility of all, children have to learn about responsibility, it is educational, it teaches the power of community.

A little bit from everybody achieved a lot. Compare a bit of turf (or wood) each day to the present situation of all the oil-powered central-heated schools across the country. The heat is a direct expense to be borne by the state paid-for with our taxes. The oil comes out of the ground half the way round the world, it is shipped in huge tankers, is processed, shipped again, arrives in Ireland, onto tankers plying our road system to centralized storage facilities, back onto tankers, and arrives at the school. Any 'sustainable' alternatives around seem to suffer from the same malaise, pellet boilers, geo-thermal systems, all require distribution systems, pellets from afar, or electricity from the grid and complex technology requiring installation and maintenance by experts, all out of the control of the school community.

The closest school-heating system to the turf-in-the-pocket system has been developed in Finland where a local farmer wins a contract to heat local schools or nursing homes using timber from local forestry. Instead of selling fuel he or she is selling heat, value is added, transport costs are at a minimum and someone within the school community is benefiting. This model is being introduced into Ireland by the County Clare Wood Energy Project. Three suppliers have set up and been awarded contracts, and early indications are that heat is being supplied at 35 per cent of what oil would cost. *art centre ?*

Fiona Woods is the driving force behind the Ground-Up Collective. This artist-led co-operative society, also centred in Co. Clare, though involving international artists and art agencies, seeks to make art that is generated out of small rural communities, and whose audience is that same community.

In effect Ground Up was initiated to challenge the assumption that rural audiences could make do with the 'traditional' arts, while new, challenging contemporary work, could only be appreciated by urban audiences, viewed in art 'centres'.

What the collective is challenging is in effect the typical situation that the rural-based artist places themself in. Art follows an accepted model where the artist thrives on the *tranquillity and beauty* of a rural setting, withdrawn from *society* (urban that is), they live as an outsider, make art which none of their neighbours understands or appreciates, and then they bring it to a gallery in a city to sell. A completely suburban (in essence) lifestyle, which does little to enrich their local community and is so committed to the primacy of the urban audience. As Woods describes it, 'the destruction of locality where all your dealings are with the city'.

As in any centralized system, the art power, the buyers and critics, the galleries and museums are all urban based. If work is to challenge this system it has to operate outside of galleries which most of their intended rural audience would never enter. Artists living in rural areas all benefit from interacting with their communities, as people as much as artists. In the words of one of the ground-up artists, Vincent Wall, 'The artist is just another personality, and a community is made up of lots of personalities.' Rural populations are often termed 'uneducated' in terms of culture, but the artists involved in their communities often testify to how much they are indeed learning from their neighbours. The artist introduced into this existing rural community structure by definition becomes important at some level to everyone—either in what they make or what they say or simply what they are. What they make, or do needs to be manifest in the community.

If Ground up could be said to be challenging the centralized system of art, and indeed culture that exists at present, what are the alternatives ? Can culture exist across a network ? Does it remain cutting edge ?

internet

The internet is obviously the most important contemporary manifestation of a networked system. The way it is being used optimizes on that connectivity which allows a multitude of people to create a single entity together, a bit like all the termites working on their termite mound. One example of this is the *Wiki*. A Wiki allows anyone viewing a site to also change or update any page online in a browser, or add a page of their own, thus the wiki is the platform for online collaboration. The first Wiki was developed in 1995 by Ward Cunningham, a software engineer who set out to develop something that would allow groups to collaborate on software code, simultaneously publish their efforts and document any changes made. There are now many *wikis*, a lot of them are used as a database and idea-swapping mechanism by software engineers, the first people to really understand the implications of the internet (followed closely, it seems, by teenagers). The most popular wiki is Wikipedia, the vast on-line encyclopedia. So many people use Wikipedia now as a resource they forget that it was built from the ground up by volunteers and by its users, all remote geographically from one another yet contributing to a single entity that continues to grow and change, in the hands of anyone who bothers to submit material. It is the largest ever encyclopedia, with 1.6 million articles, and 27,000 people making at least three edits per year. It relies crucially on peer-review publications not personal authority.

rural networks

Whether energy, art, politics or information it seems that the possibilities of the network as an organizational principle are huge. It is a system that is fundamental to how nature operates, how we operate. It allows a sophistication of result through simple means reliant on a community of interested people, as opposed to external experts. The development of technological networking like the internet gives a new possibility of connectivity, and compliments the small, tight-knit groupings which we associate with the best communities, with another larger scale of on-line community that fosters innovation and creativity.

bungalows, bungalows, bungalows

Whenever I find myself within a group of dubliners, The Big Bungalow Question comes up, I suppose because I would be considered, as an urban architect who has moved to the country, to be the voice of reason and taste in a rural world gone mad—until the publication of this book at least.

New houses in rural areas receive a lot of criticism in the press and from environmentalist groups. We hear that they are 'ugly', 'tasteless', 'badly sited', 'unsustainable' and that there are altogether too many of them—a 'bungalow blitz'. This criticism tends to be a potent mixture of superficial and studied, subjective and valid, but whatever it is, it always seems to come from an urban perspective—is there a rural perspective worth listening to ? In terms of habitat as in terms of culture it seems that urban Ireland considers that the rural masses are in dire need of education.

The solutions offered are inevitably control through legislation.

We have a habit in the modern world, when we are being a little lazy perhaps, of looking at the symptoms of problems, and just dealing with them and not the root cause—this is exactly how the bulk of quick-fix, patient-as-consumer, modern Western medecine operates. Do you have a headache ? Just take a pain killer. If everything looks good on the surface we are happy and any side-effects can be further treated by another drug. Common sense must tell us that this approach causes huge problems in the long term, in the area of health, for example, serious illness and depression.

The attempts to control rural development by planning legislation have been to date rather disastrous. On the one hand they are not carrying out their stated objective of 'controlling' development and on the other they are alienating a generation of rural dwellers.

They are looking at the symptoms and ignoring the underlying causes.

usury—who stole our homes (and our freedom) ?
Architects are responsible for helping people join the most important system of control of our times : The Mortgage.

Usury was considered a sin in the the Christian church up until the Reformation, as Thomas of Cobham, a thirteenth-century monk recorded, 'it is clear that the usurer cannot be considered a sincere penitent unless he has returned everything that he extorted through the sin of usury'.

Usury, in the form of the mortgage, has become the prime mechanism of control today, owning property comes with the promise of liberty, yet delivers slavery. In our modern society the idea that the house is our home, a place to love and to care for, to feel safe in, to express our lives in, is all but forgotten. It has been replaced by notions of investment, maintenance-free finishes, a step on the *ladder*. Estate agents rule. Notions of home have been replaced by ideas about property, home as commodity, and these ideas place people in a situation of debt throughout their working lives, where they must before anything else, pay their monthly mortgage installments, or else lose their house. This means that you become a willing slave, scared of losing your job, obedient to the boss, under constant financial stress, yet a valuable part of a system which values GNP over quality of life.

Each time a house is built in Ireland what are we getting? Why did we build it? The average house curently costs €300,000. All told with vat, development levies, stamp duty, income tax, PRSI and corporation tax, the government pockets about €100,000, and gets a willing slave for the length of their mortgage, someone who must toe the line and stay in a job or lose their house (*see* www.finfacts.com). The escape route, winning the lottery, is nothing but a disguised further tax on your income.

It looks to me as if the primary purpose of house building is economic, the development of our economy marches on, the qualities of home forgotten.

No wonder the resulting houses aren't pretty.

meitheal

The houses that people like in the countryside are the old cottages. Despite being a bit dark and damp people think that they are quaint, they seem nestled into their site, they have gentle rounded corners, and big generous fireplaces, all in all they seem homely, familiar. The thatched cottage is imbedded in the collective consciousness of our society as the architypical comfortable house. How did these houses come into being, who built them?

85

These houses were built by the people who were going to live in them with the help of friends and neighbours. The site was carefully chosen by people who knew the area very well. It was important that it did not sit on good agricultural land, but the site did have to be as dry as possible. It had to be sheltered, and close to a source of water, well or stream. A lot of time, thinking, talking, debating and reflection went into choosing a suitable site. The building work was carried out by a *meitheal*, a collective of local people whose lives were made easier and more fun by sharing the bigger tasks. *Meitheals* were used to make hay, bring in the harvest and other such things, and though people worked hard, there was also music, singing and a party afterwards organized by the recipient of the help. Thus foundations were laid, walls built of stone or mud depending on local availability. Some jobs were more specialized. Each locality would have a thatcher to both thatch the new house and carry out maintenance work on the existing housing stock. He was kept busy on roofs in good weather, and preparing materials in bad. Building was a challenge, a joy and something that brought everyone together. In the words of J.M. Synge talking about thatching a house on the Aran islands, 'from the moment a roof is taken in hand there is a whirl of laughter and talk till it is ended, and, as the man whose house is being covered is a host instead of an employer, he lays himself out to please the men who work with him'.

The character of a society's houses are intertwined with the character of that society. Real Beauty in a building is never skin deep, never just the result of good design, it is always the manifestation of a more fundamental quality, something tied back to the beliefs and aims of the society that built it.

development

When did we begin to change our relationship with our home and our landscape ? In trying to examine the basis of the modern wave of development in rural Ireland, I started by going back to look at what drives 'development' and how this has affected recent Irish history. The late 1950s and early 1960s is the key time. This is when Ireland first started to receive Marshall Aid, an American aid program. Prior to its arrival on these shores, Ireland was pursuing its own individual economic policy. Driven by Eamonn DeValera, it centred on self sufficiency and the development of indigenous resources and ran counter to the global orthodoxy at the time which would, in the future, drive globalization as we know it today. In return for Marshall Aid, Ireland was encouraged to introduce a neo-Keynesian orthodoxy to economic planning. What were the purposes of the 'economic development' that Marshall Aid was assisting ?

> Economic development of an underdeveloped people by themselves is not compatible with the maintenance of their traditional customs and mores. A break with the latter is prerequisite to economic progress. What is needed is a revolution in the totality of social, cultural and religious institutions and habits, and thus in their psychological attitude, their philosophy and way of life. What is, therefore, required amounts to social disorganisation. Unhappiness and discontentment in the sense of wanting more than is obtainable at any moment is to be generated. The suffering and dislocation that may be caused in the process may be objectionable, but it appears to be the price that has to be paid for economic development: the condition of economic progress.' from an article by J.L. Sadie, 'The social anthropology of economic development', *Economic Journal* no. 70, 278, June 1960. Quoted in *Soil and Soul* by Alastair McIntosh (Aurum Press Ltd 2001)

We reap many obvious benefits from our new-found prosperity in Ireland, and this prosperity must in part be due to Marshall aid and subsequent EU membership.

However, it is also true that we are still living in this society where 'wanting more' has become a way of life, and we have become blind to the 'suffering and dislocation' visited upon us by aggressive politics of growth. Luckily for Ireland, where we all but avoided the earlier havoc caused by the new working habits heralded in by the industrial revolution, another way of life is firmly in the living memories of older generations, and as we examine the positive aspects of this life, and realize that the grinding poverty that was experienced is mutually exclusive from the 'good old days' that my neighbours reminisce about. We must learn from the past intelligently. We must not throw the baby out with the bath water.

designing communities

Instead of building *houses* and *developments* we need to concentrate our energies on making homes and communities. People make communities, and when you examine communities that have evolved slowly the built framework that allows the community to happen is just right. Sometimes this just evolves yet sometimes it has been designed. Humankind has thresholds of comfort with regard to association with others and privacy, these thresholds are very adaptable and change from culture to culture and from individual to individual. This is the instinct that comes into play when you go to the beach, you have a sense of how close you may sit beside another family group to allow privacy but allow the future possibility of an exchange, you can study first hand the cultural differences to this sense when you observe for example how the German family sitting uncomfortably (for us) close to their sunbathing neighbour has a different sense of space.

It is difficult to design buildings in which community is guaranteed to happen, so many factors come into play, there is so much to get wrong, and small differences have big impacts. I recently re-visited two buildings that the architecture firm of Leipe and Steigelmann, where I worked, built in Berlin in the early 1990s. They were both similar in design, each having about twelve apartments that opened from a central glazed court. Along with my ex-boss Hartmut Steigelmann we spent an afternoon knocking on doors and chatting to the residents who had been mostly there for about ten years. What became apparent was that one of the buildings had a happy active community that organized house parties, checked in on each other, swapped babysitting, it was a building that exuded warmth and happiness. The other building (the one that I had worked on) had had more tenants come and go over the years, people did not really have much to do with their neighbours. We talked to people about this, and we discovered that the deciding difference in the two buildings was that in the first you could only enter each flat by walking through the central glazed court and up the central open staircase, in the less successful building the stairs is tucked away (we thought it looked better like that), which meant that people weren't forced to socialize and they never got to know each other.

This is what makes it so difficult for architects to design functioning communities from the top down, why the twentieth century is littered with failures. Community is a volatile thing, and one that is best allowed to evolve, it is something that architects seem not to be good at designing on their own.

WALTER SEGAL

Walter Segal was born in Hungary in 1907 and grew up in Switzerland, he studied architecture in the Bauhaus in Berlin and left for London in 1936 as the Nazis came into power. He became disenchanted with the normal structures of architectural practice, unhappy with the architect/client/builder relationship which is so fraught with

89

strife and unhappiness. In 1960 he decided to refurbish his home in London, and built a light-weight timber house in his garden to house his family while the re-building work was carrying on. They in fact never moved back into the original house and the timber-frame house is still there 47 years later. Through this experience he developed a system of timber-frame building which anyone could do, through a careful examination of the building process and simplifying it down to 17 core skills so that his clients could build their own buildings. This led to happy clients and then on eventually to public commissions : Social-housing projects for local councils first in the London Borough of Lewisham in 1976 and then throughout England. These consisted of groups of six to ten houses built by their future occupiers with council-purchased materials who came from the council waiting lists. Ken Atkins of the Lewisham Self-Build Housing Association describes the achievement of building his own house as the 'indescribable feeling that you finally have control over what you are doing.' They have been a resounding success in terms of building stable communities, in providing disenfranchized members of society with renewed confidence, and in architectural design. Since Walter Segal's death in 1985 his work has been carried on by many younger architects and is supported by the Walter Segal Self-build trust.

What happens in these developments is that everybody gets to know each other during building, problems arise and have to be sorted out, people learn to rely on each other a bit. A community is forged from a disparate collection of individual families. As the architects involved in designing the projects are passionate about the idea of *community architecture* they put lots of energy in getting it right and have learned the skill of letting the community lead. It is perhaps not by chance that Jose Ospino, one of the central driving members of CHISEL the housing co-operative that has built many

Segal-style developments across the South of England during the early 1990s hails from South America and is well versed with the inspiring work of Paulo Freire.

If we put an historical understanding like meitheal together with modern techniques like Walter Segal's building system, and an understanding of townland and clachan as appropriate scales of operation we start to see the possibilities of a development of communities as opposed to the development of profit.

CONCLUSION

The rural landscape is not a museum, not a picture postcard. It is at present an underused, neglected and misunderstood resource, its pleasures, advantages, its complete necessity forgotten and lost in our headlong rush to a mediocre, car-dependent suburban existence. It is almost by definition misunderstood, as the experts that form policy, that make the big decisions, are mostly urban based, suburban-dwelling people for whom the rural is a memory, the past, or an idle weekend away.

To me it seems that Ireland has luck on its side. A sophisticated rural *modus operandi* existed until quite recently, and though our society has been hurt and damaged by the aggressive forces of economic growth, a strong sense of another life exists in living memory, it is enshrined in our constitution and indeed this other life is still being practiced by many older people, and younger new rural dwellers.

In a time of rising energy prices and long-term oil depletion we have a lot to learn, or relearn about our landscape. Food and energy security will become national imperatives. Rural Ireland is going to become an essential resource, a provider of food and energy to a growing Irish population. This will require a much bigger rural population, and a new way of housing that population and of farming that is economic, fosters community and co-exists with the other natural systems around it.

Top-down, large-scale decision making produces mediocrity and a sense of hopelessness in communities removed either geographically or economically from the seats of power. The local must regain prominence as the primary organizing principle, decision-making basis and the primary market. A new dynamic infrastructure will be used to service this rural population, this growth in rural population to counteract oil peak is not a 'backward slide' rather it is a re-balancing that allows people a richer, healthier and more varied life, that can heal the social and medical ills being experienced in Ireland, while capitalizing on the changes that are happening in work structures. We can regain the pleasure of the tight-knit community of the past, without the poverty which we in Ireland associate with that existence.

The State shall, in particular, direct its policy towards securing that there may be established on the land in economic security as many families as in the circumstances shall be practicable.

Irish Constitution Article 45.2v

build

built with our hands

We inhabit the site slowly, learning its routes, winds, shelter and views. First in tents and temporary structures, then in a frame in which we place the stuff of permanent living. As we build, a condensed history, a dense system of memories is established. An intense rite of passage, like the birth of a child, binding us to the emerging house.

Forty-four days later, two weather-proof timber boxes, anchored beside existing blackthorn trees. The days get shorter and as we discover what the essentials of living really are we make divisions, doors, objects to suit our needs. We learn about the necessity of comfort.

Responding to the complexities of use, within a thick insulating strawbale wall protecting us from the North, connections between rooms, thresholds, inbetween spaces emerge, ambiguous spaces waiting to be named and for a pattern of use to settle on them.

Building one's own house is a vernacular tradition almost lost in most rural communities in Ireland. It makes dreams obtainable, an empowering yet economically pragmatic experience.

spaces for living
There are two different kinds of spaces in this home, drawing on different traditions and fulfilling different needs.

The first sit within the timber frame. Two horizontal planes sail above the landscape. Between this floor and ceiling happen specific functions: cooking, eating and sleeping. These rooms are four sided, the edges defined by walls or floor-to-ceiling glazing. We built these clear, simple rooms first. They sit as clear hand-made structures within their natural surroundings.

The second kind of space is earth bound. The floor runs with the landscape, the thick walls imply excavated space, the spaces formed are ambiguous—are you within the wall or beside it? These have become known as inbetween spaces, where the unprogrammed activity of life can happen. You can loiter, sit undisturbed in the corner reading a book, gaze into the fire. These are places to withdraw from the world, to feel protected, it is as if you are enveloped within the landscape itself.

low technology
Mari-aymone and I designed this home so that we could build it ourselves. It is built of local materials, using constructional logic that combines the modern with the vernacular.

The frame—inspired by Walter Segal—was fabricated on site in our polytunnel workshop. Its grid size suits 1220x2440 mm sheet sizes, allowing just-in-time decision-mak-

ing with regards to envelope and internal features. The façades are essentially curtain walling, glazing fixed to timber struts with aluminium cover profiles. The cladding is palette wood: after its 5-10 year life span it will be burnt in the stove, the building getting a fresh skin.

The strawbale walls are rendered inside and out with a thick lime plaster. A system of blockwork internal partitions support the roof, which was in place before delivery of the strawbales. The strawbale walls act as a non-structural screen wall, stack-bonded and strapped to the concrete block at intervals.

This approach to technology has resulted in a per-square-metre building cost of only €600, including services, site works and all finishes.

low energy
Warmth in Winter, ventilation in Summer, it is important to achieve these passively in a house.

The house has two modes of environmental operation. In the winter the extensive south-facing glazing admits any sunlight available. This heats up the massive North side of the house. Super insulation of the rest of the envelope guards against excessive heat loss. In the summer large openings on the west and east elevations admit a gentle breeze to cool the house during long hot summer days a continuous process of reflection and learning fuelled by building and living.

area : approx. 200m² (fluctuating)
work in progress since 1999

N

103

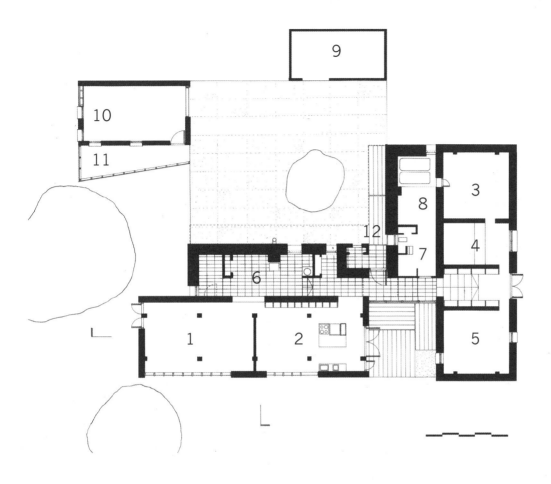

1	living
2	kitchen
3	dressing
4	sleeping
5	sleeping
6	sitting
7	toilet/shower
8	bathing
9	store
10	studio
11	greenhouse
12	entrance

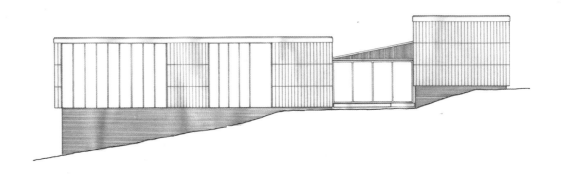

107

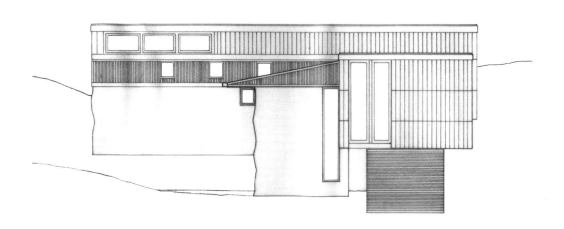

A momentary angular deformation of the landscape around it, the house sits in its surroundings like a passing shadow. You approach the house across a field, you enter down a cutting, the entrance ravine, where hillside becomes front door. The house doesn't alter the landscape in which it sits, rather, the constantly changing landscape alters the house.

earthwork and framework
There are two types of spaces in this house. You enter into the ground itself, buried, protected, space within the landscape. Earthworks. From here you travel up the spiral staircase, spun around, re-orientated, you rise up onto a platform. Reintroduced to the landscape through the filter of the façade, the surrounding hills are viewed as picture, captured by the house. The space of this four-sided room is specific, its deformations

111

question your sense of scale, your judgement of three dimensions. This white space is a secret lodged in the middle of the field, a protected habitat concealed by surface as opposed to form.

living and working
The site retains its agricultural function, producing food and fuel as it has done for hundreds of years. It is home and studio for two conceptual artists who work from different spaces at different times. Small computer workstations tucked into corners in the earthworks below, and the large flexible space upstairs good for spreading things out, for the stuff of general living, and parties.

economic
It is essential for society, and for the individual householder that architecture is not seen as a luxury item, that design is not a thing that is priced only for the rich.

The mimetic house was built for just €1000 per square metre. This is as cheap as a suburban semi-detached house.

area : 120 m²
design to completion : 2002–06

114

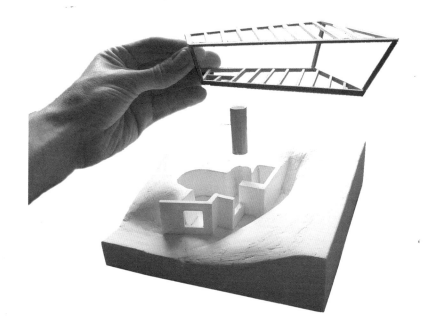

framework

connector

earthworks

115

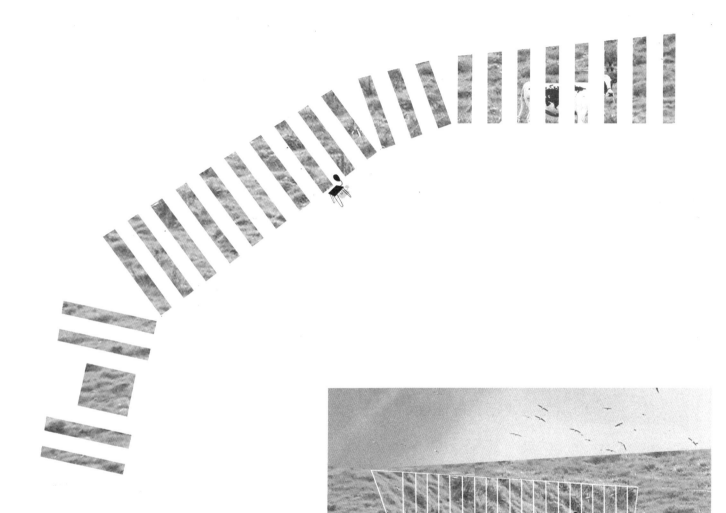

117

118

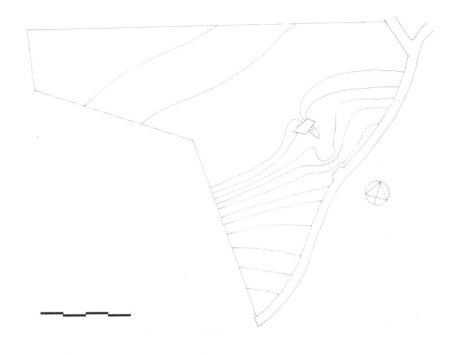

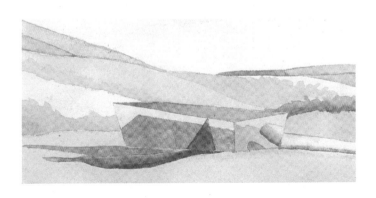

119

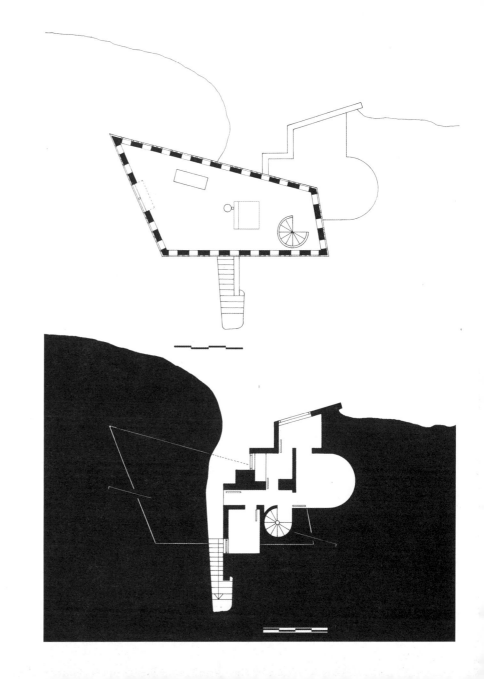

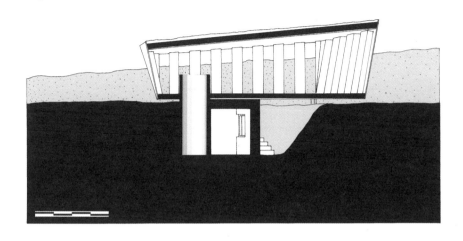

123

The circulation spaces, the leftover spaces, the common spaces in buildings, are where the user finds an open programme, a temporary void in time, space and function. these spaces lie inbetween defined spaces of activity. Children are sent to school to sit in classrooms and learn, yet it is in the corridors that they acquire their most valuable skill—how to negotiate society. Ultimately, in the inbetween spaces, it is up to you to take control and decide what to do. What better place to read than on the stairs ?

house
This house is for a couple who work from home, and their two children. They decided to move from central Dublin to a hillside overlooking a lake in Leitrim. The house has two kinds of spaces. The first has distinct functions—sleeping, cooking, working, bathing—each in a separate block. These rooms are a defined shape : They have four

walls ; you know whether you are within the room or outside it ; they envelop and protect you. Their individual shapes force you to be aware of the walls, the edges of the enclosure. They require conscious evaluation of shape and size. The windows and doors in these walls give framed views of the landscape. Between these rooms flows an inbetween living/connecting space. It is in this inbetween space that the unprogrammed activity goes on, the general stuff of living. These all flow into one another. How they are used is reinvented day after day. Hillside becomes entrance space becomes reading corner becomes gathering space. These are spaces that, although charged with atmosphere, are not particular in their suggested use—like a forest clearing or a hilltop plateau.

place in the landscape
The house is made of pieces that have a scale and material simplicity akin to rural Irish vernacular houses. This collection of pieces sits in the landscape like a traditional settlement of house and outbuildings. The pieces capture a fluid moment in the landscape—a collection of terraces where the inbetween space happens.

area : 200 m²
completed : 2003

128

129

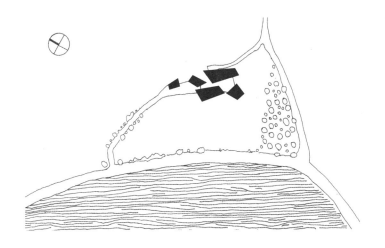

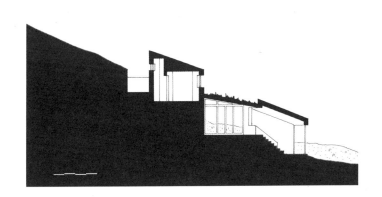

131

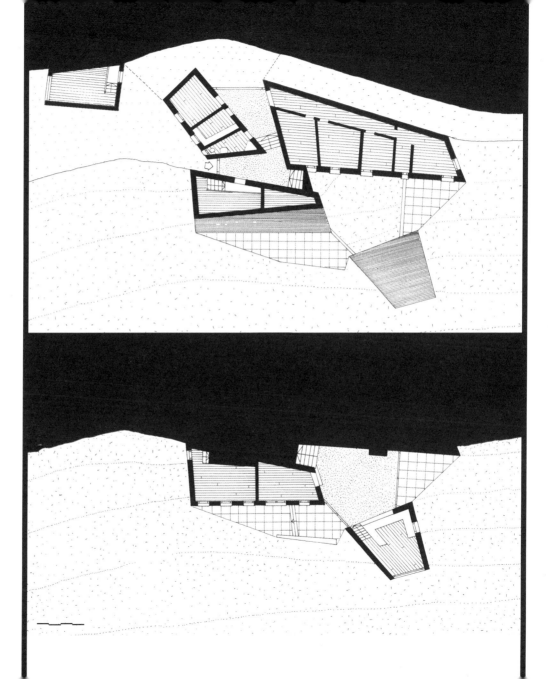

The hide-and-seek house is situated in a tough west-of-Ireland landscape of high winds, sheeting rain, but also of great beauty.

In order to survive in this landscape the house is conceived as a strong, simple and dependable object. Squat and hunched down against the wind, its forms are reminiscent of the simple vernacular houses of this windswept region.

Once inside the hard external skin, the house becomes a complex internal world that enjoys the world outside but is protecting and comfortable. It encloses many different types of spaces, this allows my clients, a couple who work at home a lot, and their young children, to all find their own spaces to do different things come rain, hail or sunshine.

Relaxing
An enclosing, encircling living space with library mezzanine. From this room the views out to the landscape are like a captured image, a beautiful picture seen at a remove.

Viewing

Casemates are rooms that are built within the thickness of the external walls. In the casemates the view becomes dominant, you are still inside, yet sitting within the view. These casemates give a visual threshold between room and landscape.

Sleeping

Buried bedrooms with sea views.

Playing outside

The captured outside space, rooflit and south facing, contains a patio, garden shed and a south-facing wall to sit against and enjoy the sun, all year round. It protects the house from the buffeting of the southwest prevailing wind. This reduces heat-loss, and its south-facing rooflights capture heat from the sun.

Working

An office space within the overall house volume yet with a separate entrance.

area : 260 m²
completed : 2007

138

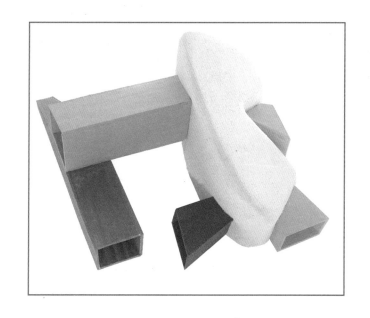

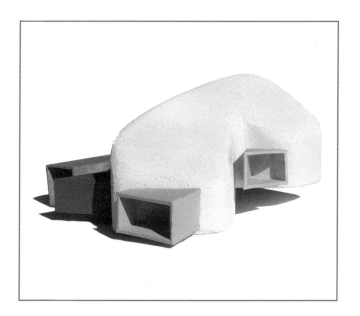

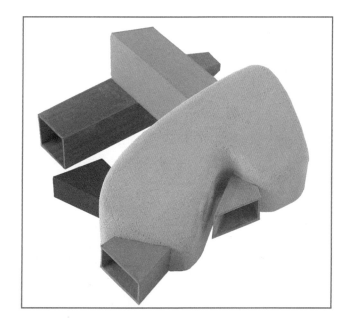

141

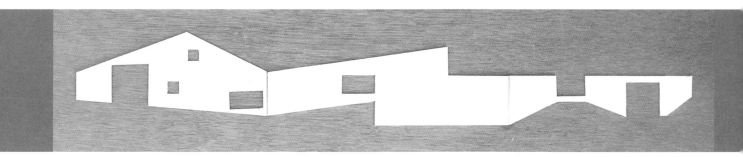

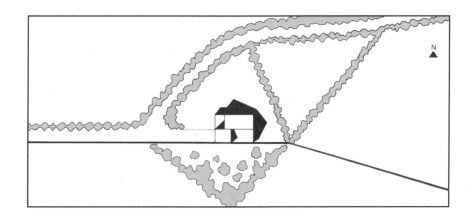

143

main floor

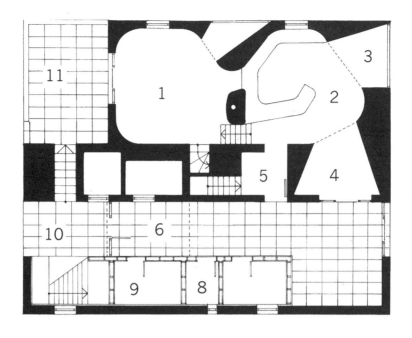

1	living
2	kitchen
3	dining
4	playing
5	hall
6	inside/ outside
7	utility
8	bathroom
9	store
10	porch
11	terrace

145

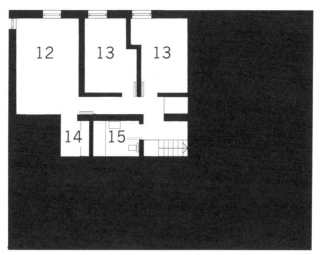

lower level

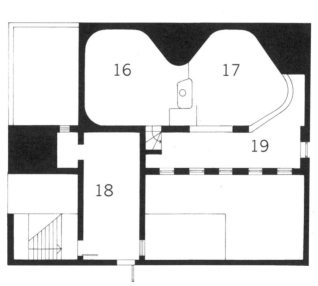

upper level

12	sleeping
13	sleeping
14	dressing
15	bathing
16	living height
17	kitchen height
18	office
19	library

147

The fields between the lakes are small, separated by thick hedges of whitethorn, ash, blackthorn, alder, sally, rowan, wild cherry, green oak, sycamore, and the lanes that link them under the iron mountains are narrow, often with high banks. The hedges are the glory of these small fields, especially when the hawthorn foams into streams of blossom each May and June.

Memoir, John McGahern

Hedgerow

This South Leitrim landscape of small fields surrounded by thick hedges, somehow survived the ravages of EU-inspired field-enlargement destruction. The land that this house sits on is made up of 7 acres divided into 10 fields. Each field has its own character, as if rooms of a house, and just as in a house as you progress deeper into the site the level of privacy increases.

The house takes the form of the hedgerows, thus becoming a part of the edge to four fields instead of standing as an object in space. Just as hedgerows, the house sits as a divider, a surface in the landscape as opposed to a form. Rooms address different fields, each room absorbing the character of the field that it overlooks.

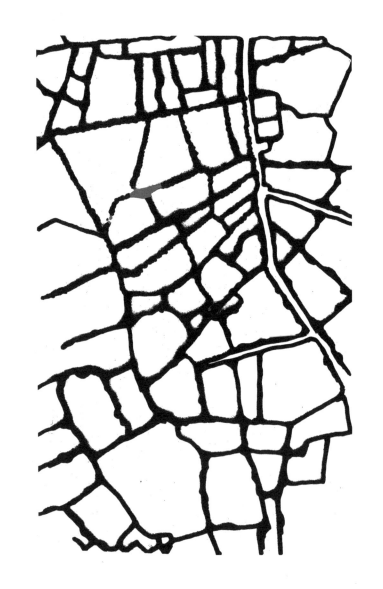

Living outside

My clients, a couple with no children, were living in an old cottage, which in common with most cottages was damp and enclosed. Like a lot of my neighbours they spent a lot of time outside, and had erected a pergola with glazed roof adjacent to their cottage. Ireland has a very mild climate, you can spend most of the time outside if you are sheltered from the rain and the wind, and this outside life was to be preserved in the new house.

Productive landscape

The site is 7 acres. This area of land suits an approach to food, heating and energy : instead of relying on complex technology to heat the house, 4 acres are being planted with mixed forestry to supply timber which will in time stock the houses 3 masonry stoves, which in tandem with passive-solar gain will heat the heavily insulated house with ease. Food is to be produced on site, and we are exploring the use of a combination of wind turbines and solar panels to harvest electricity supply.

Adaptive

The house changes with the seasons, just as hedgerows do.

In the winter the external skin of glass and translucent GRP is closed, protecting the wintergardens from cold temperatures, the thick strawbale insulating walls from rain while admitting passive-solar gain which is absorbed by the thick concrete deck and lime-rendered walls, thus this buffer zone lessens heat loss from the heated volumes in the house, and is a nice place to sit out on many winter days.

In the summer the external skin slides away as needed, allowing a sheltered sundeck, shading the rooms from the hot midday sun and connecting easily with the surrounding landscape.

154

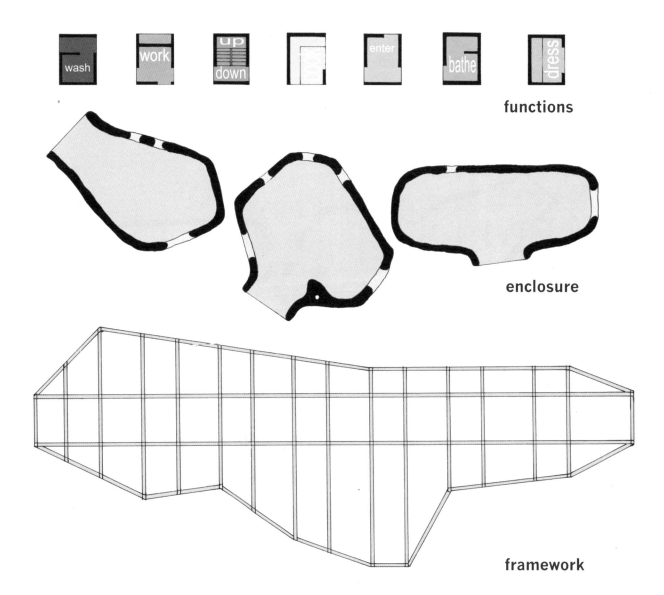

wash work up down enter bathe dress

functions

enclosure

framework

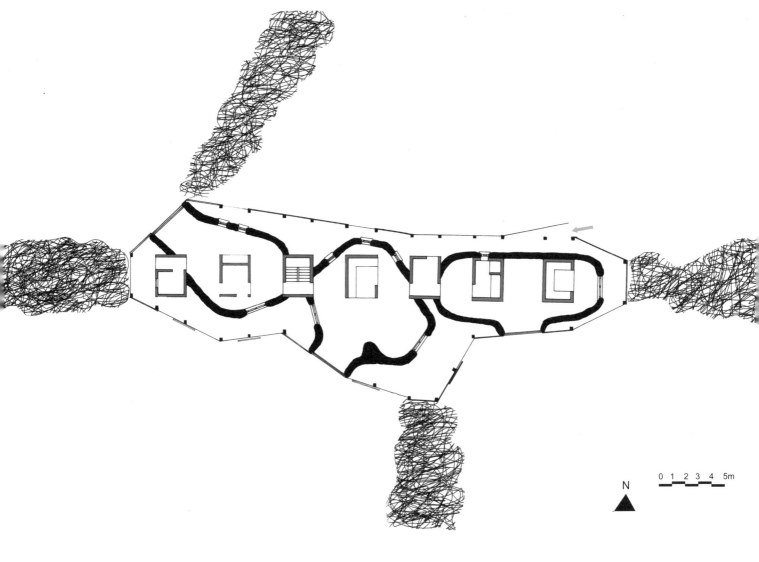

area : 165 m² plus 145 m² sundecks and verandas.

157

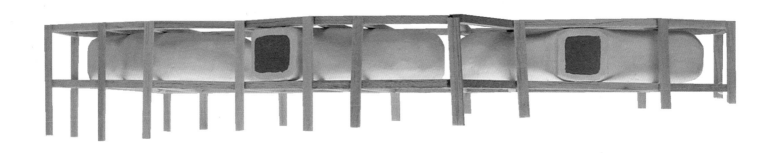

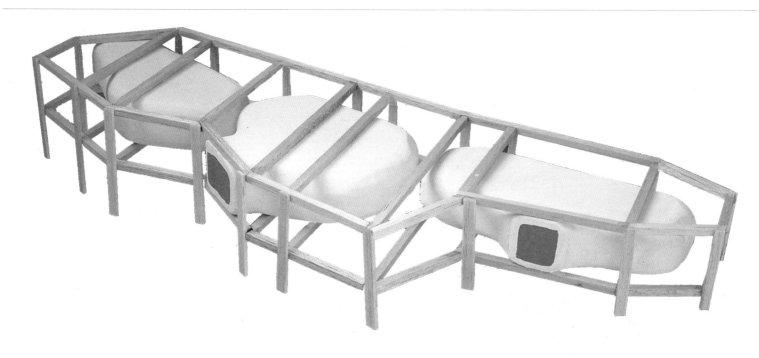

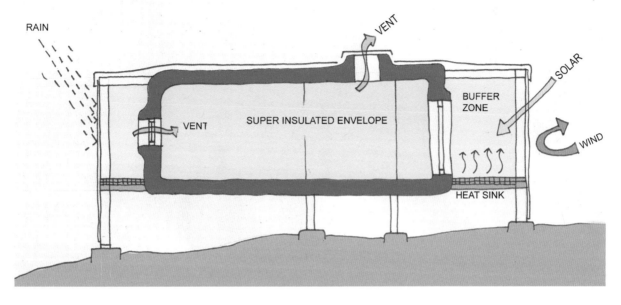

RAIN

VENT

VENT

SUPER INSULATED ENVELOPE

BUFFER ZONE

SOLAR

WIND

HEAT SINK

159

plan

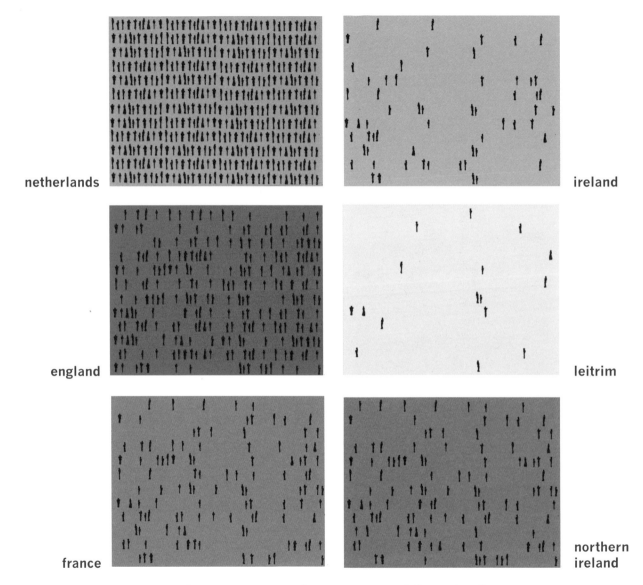

netherlands

ireland

england

leitrim

france

northern ireland

how many people per square kilometre ?

size, density, growth
Ireland is in a unique situation within Europe. We are a small country of about 5 million people with population densities far lower than the European norm, yet with a proportionally large projected population growth over the next 25 years of 1 million. An even larger growth is possible and desirable if we first recognize, then manage and market our assets to an increasingly unstable world.

skills, past and present
We have no history of industry and manufacturing, rather our history lies in small-scale agriculture and our current economic success is based on high technology and services.

opportunity

Our low-base population densities mean that at a time when food and energy security start to become political imperatives we in Ireland actually have the natural resources and skills to be energy and food self-sufficient for our current and future population, while maintaining a skilled workforce producing high technology (hardware and software) and services for export, real or virtual.

heritage

We are lucky in Ireland to have beautiful rural landscape which, apart from our recent economic boom, is our most famous asset. Following the motto, *the only way to protect heritage is to increase it*, I propose a settlement that through its proximity to nature can be energy and food self-sufficient at a local level, yet has the population densities to offer the social and cultural advantages normally associated with urban life, within a rural setting.

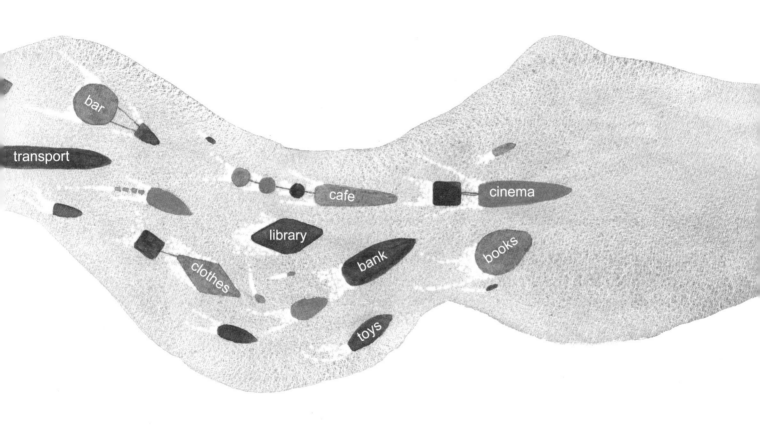

The Shannon river

The waterways in Ireland—the rivers, canals and lakes, more than 1000km in total length—are under used. I propose a vibrant, intensive linear settlement along banks of the Shannon-Erne system, which is 278 km long, with 800 km of useable shoreline. This grand, majestic river becomes a useful, sustainable infrastructure again, a population of bank dwellers farming the river plain, and using the river as a central artery for communication.

Settlement

The flood plains of the Shannon are known as 'the callows', from *caladh*, meaning river meadow. They are up to 2km wide on each side or the river. Using less than 10 per cent of this precious natural landscape, along the banks of the river and lakes a new responsive architecture will be made. Houses that rise and fall as rivers swell and flood. The unique conditions of waterside life generating a unique new culture of settlement—new, yet based on a 5-century old tradition of flood-plain settlement.

mobile, nimble

A moving city that appears overnight then vanishes quietly, departing in the mist to a new location, an ephemeral, adaptable resource, changing in size and make up with each visit, adapting organically to the desires of the inhabitants of this fluid, linear settlement.

Though a large proportion of the new dwellings would be in a fixed position, the infrastructure of servicing will be mobile. Instead of travelling to the city, the city travels to you. Cinema, bank, shop, nightclub, art gallery, museum, everything you need or enjoy plies the river bringing the world to your door.

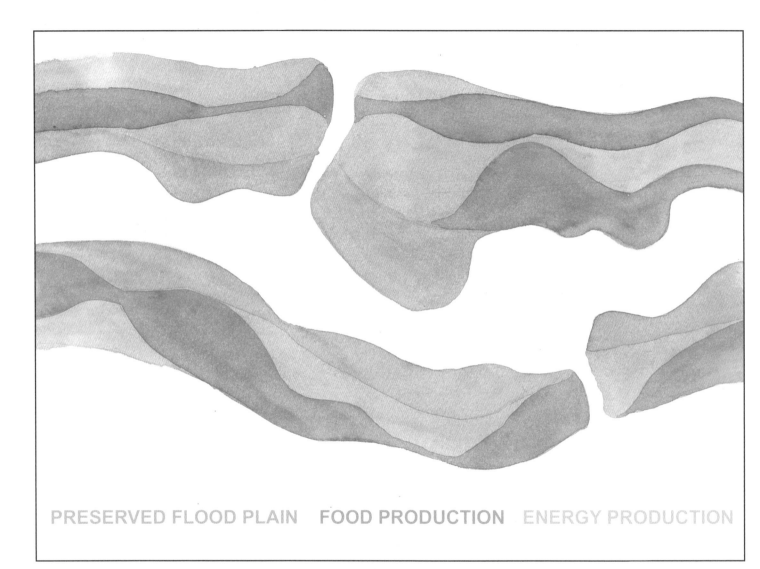

PRESERVED FLOOD PLAIN   FOOD PRODUCTION   ENERGY PRODUCTION

168

Electrical boats, batteries charged with wind, solar and water turbines, constantly on the move—the circus comes to town.

food

At present over 40 per cent of road freight is connected to the movement of food, from the land for export (93 per cent of beef produced in Ireland is exported, see p.93) and from abroad to fill our supermarket shelves. This will not be necessary in the fluidcity, where enough land for local food production, 0.3 hectare per person, which allows for non-intensive production and rotation of crops and livestock, will be set aside on the fertile river banks.

energy

In simple terms, at present, Ireland exports agricultural produce, produced uneconomically relying on heavy fossil-fuel use for machinery, fertilizers and feed production and then with the proceeds earned from these exports, we import fossil fuel. Producing food for the global market—where food prices decrease and energy prices rise—is increasingly not viable.

The new settlement will have no need for importing energy. Small-scale river turbines, and windfarms will provide local electricity needs and 0.2 hectare woodland per person will cover heating requirements. Biodiesel for boats can similarly be produced on the fertile river bank through the propagation of biomass crops.

work patterns

Repeated studies show that it is desirable to work close to your home. This brings benefits to your immediate family and to the community at large. Children gain under-

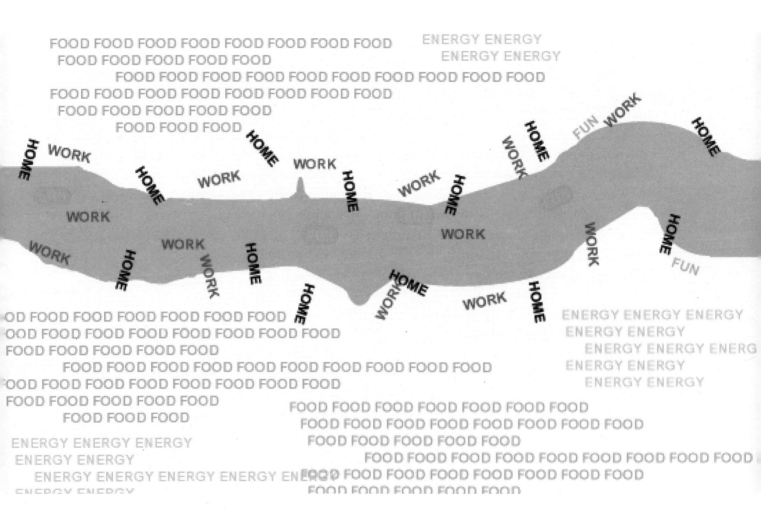

standing of what their parents do in the world of work, and the culture of the workplace becomes more a part of ordinary life—working as living not just toil. A thriving local economy is supported due to the day-round presence of everybody in the community.

The structure of work patterns have moved away from centralized production in the immense factory, away from the moving of paper up and down the corridors of large office buildings. All kinds of work from the skilled to the unskilled can happen in smaller more personable groupings. Local working therefore is full of opportunity in the fluidcity, connected to the world, high-value items travelling quickly by internet, low-value items slowly, down the river to the offshore seaports.

A mix of types of work during the day are of benefit to one's general well being. In the fluidcity a part of each day can be spent on food or energy production, though about five hours a week is all that would be necessary.

nature and a dynamic vernacular
This new settlement on the river sits on what is in part a sensitive natural habitat for many species of birds, wildlife and plant life. It achieves a density, while leaving a large proportion of the landscape of untouched, potential wilderness. It seeks to understand and work with nature, resisting our compulsive, single-minded efforts to control water through elaborate interventions, rather it will work with a dynamic relation between land, water and settlement.

The approach suggests that each geographic region can be made richer if the built is informed by the natural. This leads to a dynamic vernacular, a built environment that doesn't just co-exist with but has a symbiotic relationship with the natural.

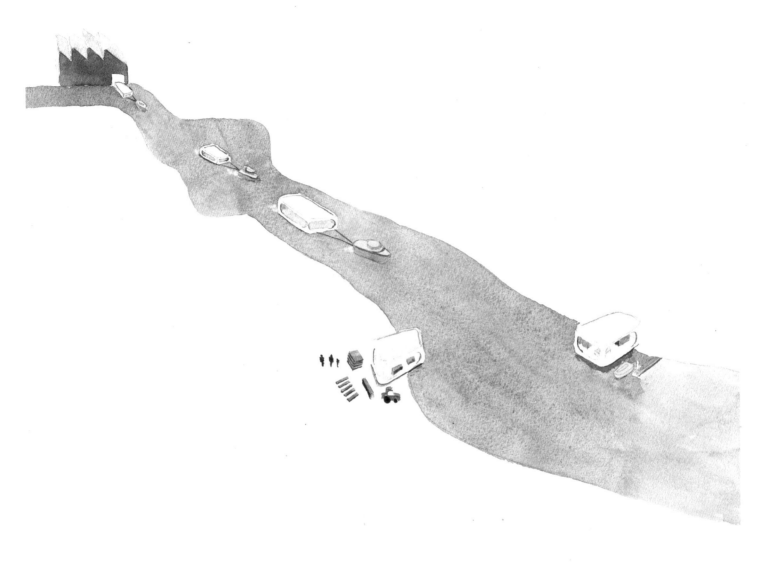

density

Along a 100m-wide strip on each side of the river, 0.5 hectare (500 m²) per person will allows for food and energy production. For each kilometre of shoreline we have an average of 200 people, thus the entire system—which has a usable shoreline of 800 km—would accomodate a population of 160,000, just under the current population of Fingal or Dún laoghaire-Rathdown.

prefabricated sites

Floating sites are prefabricated using current techniques using a foam-core encased in concrete as a building base. This base is fitted with a translucent roof producing a sheltered microclimate, where an outside life can be pursued out of the rain. The structures are towed down the river to their mooring position. Once in position they slide up and down their fixing poles as the waters rise and fall.

clustered communities

When these sites are fixed in position the dwellings and workplaces will be built by the inhabitants, the act of building facilitating in the formation of a happy community. These clusters would house 35 people, this is similar in size to the pre-land clearance rural settlement in Ireland, and to a typical Parisian or Berlin Apartment building. These clusters would include both domestic and work spaces.

Each cluster is responsible for 17.5 hectares of productive land and are guardians of extensive wilderness area.

174

critical mass

400 people per kilometre (counting both sides of river) gives us the critical mass needed for a vibrant community and the supply of essential services like schools, doctors and local shops. Within five minutes in a rowing boat you have contact with 200 people, enough to support, for example, a primary school, ten minutes in a motor boat you reach 1200 individuals, size enough for a secondary school.

plugged in and having it all

The fluidcity responds to the opportunities afforded us by electronic communication. Catering for all those people who can now find a way of working away from the traditional city, it allows them to balance that work with a bucolic life of growing food, rearing animals and chopping wood. It gives the farmer access to the excitement of the city, and the urban type the benefits of a relaxed outdoor life. In modern Ireland there exists in most of us these two now compatible sides.

I actualy made a little film to illustrate my proposal which can be seen on www. YOUTUBE.com if you search for 'Dominic Stevens Architect'.

[this project was presented at the tenth international architecture exhibition, Venice Biennale 2006, as part of 'Suburban to Superural', the Irish Exhibit, commissioned by the Irish Architecture Foundation and curated by FKL Architects.]

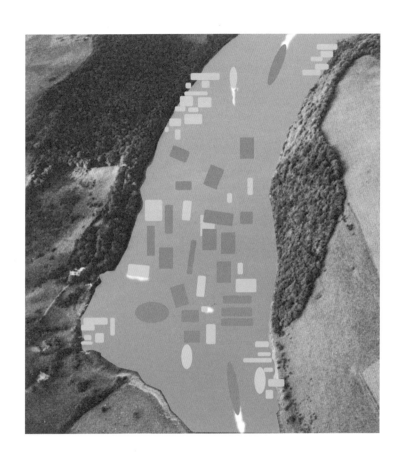

179

In 2005 I was appointed Architect in Residence by Roscommon County Council. One of my duties was to conceive a talk about building houses in rural Ireland and deliver it, followed by a discussion, in six venues around Roscommon. I did these on consecutive Wednesdays during September and October of that year.

I would roll into town with a slide projector, accompanied by Philip Delamere, the Roscommon County Council Arts Officer, acting as bodyguard, assistant, and observer. The talks took place in upstairs rooms in pubs and hotels, and as an interested group assembled we always felt like preachers from some new religion, or perhaps sellers of pyramid schemes.

My talk evidently dealt with a lot of the issues discussed in this book : how mari-ay-mone and I had built our own house and learnt in the process that we were operating within a rural tradition, how the system of inter-dependence, meitheal, bound rural communities together, and how a comparative process was being pursued in the UK through

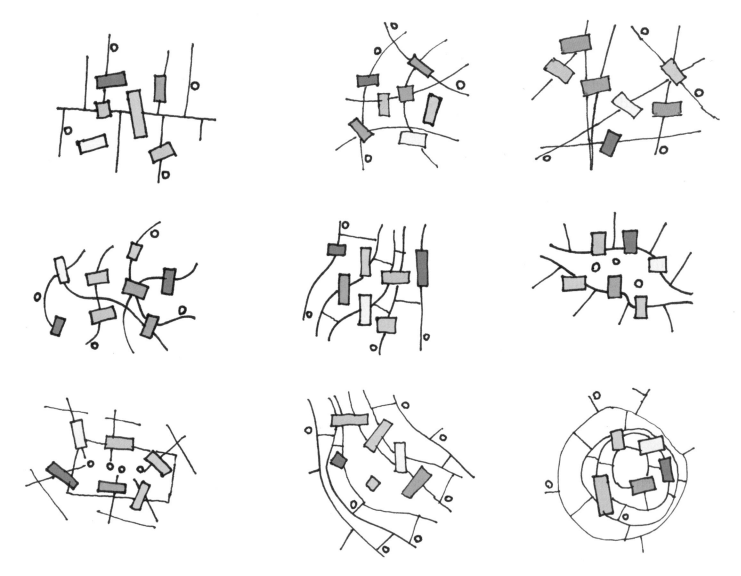

182

the work of the architect Walter Segal. This produced much discussion which sometimes carried on through the evening. It was a great opportunity for me to test-drive some of the theories and ideas I was planning to make into a book and I hope that lots of people left with new ways of looking at things, new questions in their heads (I certainly did).

The conversation continued between Philip and myself. Sitting through every single lecture, he had been rightly and willingly endoctrinated, or simply enlightened, to Walter Segal's way of building communities instead of just building houses, and he was keen to find a way to translate this into contemporary Ireland.

His determination, enthusiasm and skill, allied to the open-mindedness and forward-thinking attitudes within Roscommon County Council have given birth to a pilot project, 'The Building Communities Programme'. A feasibility study has been completed by Exodea Consulting, development consultants, examining how self-building can fit into county-council house-building programmes in terms of finance, legalities, community interest and building law. They have proven that such a programme is possible and what is being proposed is a pilot project, a group of six houses that will be self-built by people who have put their names on the housing list, on a site somewhere in county Roscommon.

For an architect a book cannot be the finished piece, that responsibility resides in an occupied building, hopefully a useful, joyful thing. It is of great comfort that even as I complete the final chapter of my book, some of the ideas that I am discussing have already leapt from the page and are becoming real tangible projects, that should benefit the people living around me, and that will hopefully fire further ideas and projects.

For a complete bibliography and a regularly updated list of further reading look at
www.mermaidturbulence.com/ruralbiblio.html
if, however, you do not have access to the internet we will be happy to it send to you by post.

photographs by Ros Kavanagh : pp. 98, 102, 104, 106, 108, 112, 114 (top left), 116, 118, 120, 122, 123, 126, 128 & 130

photographs by mari·aymone DJERIBI : pp. 50, 51, 62, 65, 138, 142 & 144 (bottom)

photographs by Paul O'Connor : pp. 114 (top right & bottom) & 146

all other photographs by dominic stevens

structural engineer (home, inbetween, mimetic & hedgerow) Casey·O'Rourke Engineers

building contractors
(mimetic and hedgerow) Greentek Ltd
(inbetween) Mac Nabola Brothers

WHAT THIS BOOK IS MADE OF

PAPER Revive 100 Offset. Fibre Source 100% post consumer waste. Pulp is bleached using a Totally Chlorine Free (TCF) process (awarded the 100% FSC recycled label and the NAPM Recycled Mark).

COVER BOARD Revive 75 Recycled Silk FSC. Fibre Source 75% post-consumer waste, 25% mill broke. Pulp is bleached using an Elemental Chlorine Free (ECF) process (awarded the NAPM Recycled Mark). FSC Mixed Sources, product group from recycled wood or fibre, well·managed forests and other controlled sources.

PAPER & BOARD produced at a mill that is certified with the ISO14001 environmental management standard.

INKS vegetable-based
Approximate ingredient percentages : 70% european-sourced soya and boiled linseed oil from commercially grown crops, small amounts of other vegetable oils are used to control the tack of the ink ; 20% Synthetic organic pigments ; 5%. Dryers (cobalt and manganese, mainly) and waxes.

LAMINATION ON COVER cellulose-based, manufactured using refined wood pulp.

CAMBRIAN PRINTERS LTD, Aberystwyth : ISO14001 and Green Dragon Level 5 certification for environmental management accredited. The company also hold FSC and PEFC chain of custody certification.

set in caslon 540 linotype, twelve on fifteen ; finished in the first days of september two thousand and seven ; printed & bound in aberystwyth by cambrian printers & published in an naghmaconway by mermaid turbulence.

mermaid turbulence

Rod Alston, Mike Burke, George Crawford, Padraig Kelly, Conor MacManus, Frank Quinn, Ezekiel Stevens, Nour Stevens, Peter Tansey, and all my clients, thank you. Thank you also to Brian Ward who worked with me in 2001.
Dominic Stevens

DOMINIC STEVENS ARCHITECT
cloone
co. leitrim
IRELAND
www.dominicstevensarchitect.com